TRAINING YOUR PET RAT

Gerry Bucsis
Barbara Somerville

BARRON'S

Dedication

This book is dedicated to Ratty, Nosey, Mischief, Scamp, Rascal, Pipsqueak, Frisk, Frolic, Frisby, Bubbles, Peaches, and Lucky—every one a winner!

Acknowledgments

Special thanks to:
- our families for their support, understanding, and encouragement.
- our editor, Anna Damaskos—more a friend than an editor.
- Diane Pawelko for all of her help and support.
- the following individuals and companies for their help and cooperation:

Absorption Corporation, Ampro Industries, The Barnaby Company, Canbrands International, Ltd., Eight In One Pet Products, Inc., Fangman Specialties, Inc., Fern Manufacturing, Gentle Touch Products, Green Pet Products, Inc., Rolf C. Hagen, Inc., Kaytee Products, Inc., Milestone Innovative Products, Mountain Meadows Pet Products, Inc., Nature's Earth Products, Inc., Paulmac's Pet Store, St. Catharines, ON (Thanks Joan and Roy!), Pen-Plax, Inc., PetAg, Inc., Petsmart, St. Catharines, ON, Pet Valu, Fonthill, ON, P. J. Murphy Forest Products Corp., "Super Pet" Pets International, Ltd., Transoniq Wodent Wheels, Vitakraft, WAL-MART Photo Finishing team, Welland, ON

Photo Credits

Cover photo: The representation of the Rubik's Cube® is used by permission of Seven Towns Ltd. Rubik® and Rubik's Cube® are registered trademarks throughout the world of Seven Towns Limited. On pages 33, 76, and on inside front cover LEGO and the LEGO logo are trademarks of the LEGO Group and are used here with special permission. Pages 39 and 93, Kladders courtesy of PetAg, Inc.; page 5, bird cage is Top Wing by Petsmart; page 12, food basket by Fern Maunufacturing; page 13, Veggie Holder courtesy of "Super Pet," Pets International, Ltd.; page 79, chewies courtesy of Rolf C. Hagen, Inc.; page 31, ferret litter pan courtesy of "Super Pet," Pets international, Ltd.; page 32, Roll-a-Nest courtesy of "Super Pet," Pets International, Ltd.; pages 35 and 44, rope bird ladder and wooden bird ladder courtesy of Rolf C. Hagen, Inc.; page 60, bird gym courtesy of PetAg, Inc.; page 61, Wodent Wheel courtesy of Transonig; page 68, ferret ball and tubes courtesy of "Super Pet," Pets International, Ltd.; pages 11 and 81, dog pull toys courtesy of Penn-Plax, Inc.; page 27, chews courtesy of Rolf C. Hagen, Inc., Kaytee Products, Inc., and Vitakraft.

All inquiries should be addressed to:
Barron's Educational Series, Inc.
250 Wireless Boulevard
Hauppauge, New York 11788
http://www.barronseduc.com

International Standard Book No. 0-7641-1208-2

Library of Congress Catalog Card No. 99-69084

Printed in Hong Kong

9 8 7 6 5 4 3 2 1

Note of Warning

This book deals with the keeping and training of pet rats. In working with these animals, you may occasionally sustain scratches or bites. Administer first aid immediately, and seek medical attention if necessary.

There are a few diseases of domestic rats that can be transmitted to humans, and some humans are allergic to rat hair and dander. If you are at all concerned that your own health might be affected, contact your doctor *before* bringing home a rat.

If your rat shows any sign of illness, be sure to visit your veterinarian.

Contents

Introduction

Are you looking for a pet that's friendly, intelligent, eager to please, and easy to train? A pet that will fit into your busy lifestyle? One that's low cost, low maintenance, and, most importantly, one that the whole family can enjoy? Then welcome to the world of the pet rat.

The pet rat??? Yes, these pint-sized pets are fast gaining in the popularity polls. At one time, rats were regarded strictly as caged pets for kids. But all that's changed. Now they're coming out of the cage and into the hearts of children, teenagers, adults, and seniors alike.

And no wonder! Rats make great pets. They're clean, they don't bark, yowl, or screech, they don't soil the sidewalks, and they don't need walks in the rain at midnight. Rats are a bargain to buy and cheap to keep. They fit into any house or apartment—if you have a place for a cage, you have a place for a rat. Best of all, they're big on personality and real people pleasers.

Do you think rats could be the right pets for you? Then you're in for a pleasant surprise. Though they're small in size, rats are big in the smarts department. Their high IQ's, combined with good memory and first-rate problem-solving skills, make them prime candidates for training...and that's where *Training Your Pet Rat* comes in. This informative, user-friendly guide will take you and your ratties through the basics of rat training and beyond. You'll learn specific techniques for teaching positive behaviors to your rats, you'll pick up tips and hints on how to tackle those annoying negative behaviors, and you'll enjoy the fun chapters on how to train your pets to perform tricks.

Why go to all the trouble of training these under-rated rodents? Well, training enhances your pets' quality of life. The learning process challenges them, stimulates them, and keeps boredom at bay. Training also enhances your enjoyment of the rats—the time you spend together gives you the opportunity to interact, to bond, and to have fun.

And after all, isn't that what pet ownership is all about?

Chapter One

Pretraining Preparations

Before you buy

Are you thinking about making a rat part of your family? Are you wondering if a rat's right for you? People who own them know that rats are good-natured pets—friendly, intelligent, and easily trained. But, before you go dashing off to buy one, find out the rat facts. Read what you can about these rascally rodents, go to the pet shop and watch their antics, talk to other owners. Then, ask yourself the all-important question—are you ready, willing, and able to give a rat pal all the care and attention it needs and deserves?

If the answer is yes, start off on the right foot by getting things ready *before* you bring one home.

The perfect house for home-schooling

The first order of business is choosing a cage. Consider yourself your rat's real estate agent. Don't make an offer on the first cage you see, because not all small animal cages are created equal. Think in terms of size—big, big, big. Why? Except for supervised play time and handling, your rat will spend much of his time in his cage. So, don't confine him to a tiny cell where cabin fever could lead to a neurotic rat. Instead, give your rat room to stretch his legs, room to burn off energy, and room for constructive play. Big cages make for happy, well-adjusted rats, and happy, well-adjusted rats are easier to train. So if you're going to splurge anywhere, it should be on housing. If money is an issue, it's better to put off your pet purchase for a while and save up the dollars for a good cage.

There are basically only two types of cage suitable for rats, aquariums and wire cages, and there are pros and cons for both types. Know the facts before you go habitat hunting.

Aquariums

On the plus side, aquariums can be found just about anywhere. They come in many different shapes and sizes, and you might even be lucky

An aquarium can be customized to make a good rat habitat.

enough to find a cheap one at a garage sale. Be aware, however, that a ten-gallon tank is the minimum size for a single rat and a twenty-gallon tank is even better. The more rats you own, the larger the aquarium needs to be. Whatever size you pick, make sure you get a ventilated, clip-on cover for the top. A cover keeps your champion high-jumper in and other pets out. If you can't find one, buy some 0.5-inch × 0.5-inch wire mesh, bend it to fit over the top, and hold it down with a heavy weight. Nix any solid covers or any with fluorescent lights. They're fine for fish but wrong for rats (gasp, gasp!).

In an aquarium, your rat will be happy because he'll have a good window on the world, he'll be cozy in the wintertime, and the glass bottom will be comfortable for his tender tootsies. You'll be happy because you'll have a good view of your rat, and he won't be able to kick out his bedding onto your floors.

Now for the downside. An aquarium big enough to provide your rat with romp room may be heavy to handle and hard to clean. If you drop it, you'll have a jigsaw puzzle that can't be put back together again. The biggest drawback to an aquarium, however, is its lack of ventilation. In the summer or in hot rooms, it can become a mini greenhouse. If it does, Ratty won't grow like a weed. Instead, he'll wilt and could even die from heatstroke. Lack of ventilation can also lead to a buildup of ammonia fumes inside the tank. These fumes, which are caused by a chemical breakdown of the rat's urine, are bad news for your buddy. Why? When he breathes them in, he can damage his respiratory system, and this, in turn, can cause chronic problems like coughing, sneezing, and shortness of breath or life-threatening problems like pneumonia. It's easy, however, to keep the fumes from forming by cleaning the aquarium thoroughly and often.

Wire cages

A wire cage can be a first-class choice for your rat's residence, but you must be picky when choosing. Before you get too excited about that large cage on special at the neighborhood pet shop, ask yourself, "Is this cage really rat friendly?"

First of all, what type of wire is it made of? Walk right past anything that's galvanized because rat urine can corrode galvanized metal. Even worse, your rat can get zinc poisoning if he chews on galvanized wire or licks his paws after climbing on it. And it's a sure bet that Ratty will lick his feet because that's how he keeps himself clean—lick, groom; lick, groom; lick, groom. So if you want a wire cage, look for one where the bars or mesh are epoxy-, vinyl-, chrome-, or powder coated. Is there anything you can do if you find that perfect cage but it's galvanized? Why not get it powder-coated? Look in the Yellow Pages under Metal Finishers. You may find someone to take on a small project.

At home in a wire cage.

Next, take a look at cage construction. Are the walls made of bars or wire mesh? In either case, check the spacing carefully. Bars should be no more than one-half inch apart because, if Ratty can get his head through, the rest of Ratty will surely follow. Wire mesh should be 0.5-inch × 0.5-inch, because no rat can escape through this size hole. Completely avoid cages with 1-inch × 0.5-inch mesh; this hole size poses a very real danger to your rats. Rats like to climb up the cage walls, and their back feet can be caught and trapped in 1-inch × 0.5-inch holes. If this happens, your pet can easily become panic stricken and injure or break a leg as he flails about trying to get free.

After you've checked the walls, it's time to zero in on the floor. Plastic is the material of choice here. It's nontoxic, foot friendly, and easy to clean. Steer clear of galvanized metal, wood, and wire. Galvanized metal can cause zinc poisoning (see page 3), so if you're going for a metal floor, look for one with epoxy or powder coating. Wood can splinter, rot, and harbor bacteria and/or fungi. Avoid it altogether. Wire flooring can trap and break fragile feet or legs. It also puts too much pressure on a rat's tender tootsies, and this can lead to bumblefoot, a painful condition of foot calluses and open sores.

A wire floor can be remodeled to be just right for your rodent by covering it *completely* with a sheet of Plexiglas cut to fit. Although Plexiglas is sturdy and long lasting, it is somewhat expensive. Cheaper alternatives would be Magic Mat from Oasis (found in pet stores) or plastic needlepoint canvas (found in craft stores). Both can be cut to fit, are washable, and are easy on rats' feet. They may, however, need to be replaced from time to time.

Most multistory cages come equipped with wire platforms. On one hand, these are great because rats love to explore different levels. On the other hand, they're not so great because wire platforms can cause the same problems as wire floors. The solution? Measure the platforms, cut Plexiglas to fit, drill a few holes along two edges of the Plexiglas, then anchor the Plexiglas to the wire shelves with florist wire. This covering makes the platforms safe and washable. A cheaper option is to buy more Magic Mat or plastic needlepoint canvas. Both can be cut to fit in minutes, and both have holes for drainage so that Ratty won't have to lie in his own puddles.

Wire ladders or ramps don't need to be given the Plexiglas treatment. After all, they're not meant to be slides, and rats don't spend much time on ladders anyway. However, if you want to play it safe, cover them with old tube socks for safer footing.

OK, you've checked the cage materials and construction, and they're right up to rat code, but you've still not finished the building inspection. Take a look at the latches. Are the doors escape proof? Or will breakouts by Ratty and break-ins by other pets be a concern? When in doubt, an inexpensive snap hook is the key to security.

A well-chosen wire cage can make a wonderful rat habitat. It's easy to handle and clean, the view is great from both inside and out, multi-level living is easy to arrange, and excellent ventilation keeps Ratty healthy.

Are there any drawbacks to a wire cage? If your house is extremely dry in the wintertime, young rats can get a condition called ringtail, where sores develop around the tail, causing constriction, scarring, and even tail loss. This problem is easily prevented by making sure the relative humidity in the rat's room is between 40 and 50 percent. A small humidifier in the room will take care of the mini-Sahara.

The most annoying problem you'll have with a wire cage is that when rowdy little Ratty is kicking up his heels, he'll also kick food and bedding onto your floors. A quick fix is to put a birdcage skirt around the bottom of the rat cage to collect the mess. Or, keep a small whisk broom and dustpan handy.

House-hunting homework

Now you know what the ideal rat lodging should look like, but finding it might not be so easy. Be prepared to do your homework. First, try your local pet store. You might find just what you're looking for, but if the ideal rat condo isn't sitting on the shelf, ask if you can order one from a supplier's catalog. However, before you place an order from any company, check the pet store's return policy on special orders.

You could also check the retail ads in small animal magazines or contact the rat organizations listed at the back of this book for specific recommendations. If you're an Internet surfer, why not get on-line and do some research? Web sites often have scanned photos and size specifications to help you with your choice.

Not just for the birds! Some bird cages make great rat roosts.

A word of warning, however. The cage that looks like a palace in a pamphlet could turn out to be too cramped for comfort. How do you avoid this pitfall? Before ordering anything sight unseen, make a mock-up cage to the exact dimensions (width × length × height) with cardboard and masking tape. Then you'll know what you're getting into—or, rather, what your rats are getting into!

Are you finding that prime rat real estate is hard to come by in your area? Perhaps it's time to take a stroll down the bird boulevard at the pet store. You never can tell—you might find the perfect rat cage masquerading as a birdcage. With birdcages, it's up to you to check very carefully for possible escape routes. After all, you don't want Ratty taking flight from his cage. So, check the wire spacing. Is it rat-proof? Are feeders part of the package? Are holes cut out for the feeders? If so, can Ratty wriggle through the space or gnaw through the plastic dishes? And don't forget to check around the pull-out tray at the bottom. Sometimes the space there is bird-proof but not rat-proof.

Birdcages are usually tall, so you'll have plenty of space to make a multilevel cage for Ratty. Check out Chapter 5 for design tips.

If you draw a blank in the bird section, the ferret section is worth a look. Ferret condos might be just the thing for large, adult male rats, but be aware that the bars in ferret cages are usually too far apart for young or female rats.

So you think that hamster habitat is a steal of a deal and cute to boot? Think again! What's homey for Hammy is wrong for Ratty. For a start, these plastic hamster homes are too small for an active rat—you don't want Ratty getting stuck in the connecting tubes. Even worse, they're not escape-proof. Ratty will soon gnaw away on the walls of the plastic modules, making exit doors wherever he chooses.

If you're into do-it-yourself projects, you might have plans to make a wooden cage. Ax the plans! Wood splinters, soaks up urine, and gets really smelly. Bacteria will have a field day, proper cleaning is impossible, and, after all your hard work, do you really want Ratty filing down his teeth on your labor of love?

Location, location, location

You've driven, searched, and surfed to find that perfect rat residence. Now, where's the best spot in your house for Ratty's house? On top of the dresser? On the rec room floor? On the desk in the den? The perfect spot in one house might not be the perfect spot in another. Look for a place that's out of the line of traffic so the cage can't be knocked around or knocked over. Just don't banish the rats to the far reaches of the house—they like to be where the action is. You want a spot where the rats are safe from the unwanted attention of other pets and small children. Add to the list a place that's normal room temperature so that your rat is warm and cozy but not too hot. It's also in your own best interest to pick a spot that lends itself to easy cleanup.

Keep the cage out of direct sunlight and away from heating vents so that Ratty won't overheat. This is especially crucial with an aquarium. Protect your pet from drafts, too, or he'll be sniffling and sneezing in no time.

Although *you* might want Ratty in the spotlight so you can watch his antics, *he'll* prefer to be out of the bright lights. Bright light can damage a rat's eyes, especially if he's an albino. So move that halogen lamp (it will overheat him anyway), adjust the miniblinds to keep out bright sunlight, or shift the cage to the shady side of the house.

When you find the perfect spot, put the cage or aquarium there, and then leave it alone. Cages aren't mobile homes, and rats aren't partial to frequent transfers.

Bedding department

Your next important decision for Ratty concerns his bedding. At first glance, there seem to be lots of choices on the pet store shelves, but some bedding is more rat friendly than others. What you're looking for is something comfy that will do a good job of soaking up Ratty's urine.

Wood shavings, chips, and pellets are readily available. They're inexpensive, fairly absorbent, and fresh smelling. A word of warning, however—soft wood products that haven't been heat treated contain a chemical (phenol) that can cause respiratory problems and possible liver damage in small animals. So for your rat's sake, stay away from cedar completely, and stay away

from pine unless it's been heat treated. Kiln-dried, compressed pine pellets such as All Pet Pine, Feline Pine, or Pine Fresh won't cause health problems for your rat, and they're excellent in the absorbency and odor-control departments. With these, you can go longer between cage cleanings.

Phenol-free hardwood products are also safe for rats. Aspen shavings and shreddings are easy to come by and reasonably priced, but they're not the best for absorbency or odor control, and they can be easily kicked out of the cage. Aspen pellets, such as Barnaby Farms Pet Bedding (also packaged as Litter Love) and GentleTouch Pet Bedding, are a better choice. They're high on the list of odor eaters; they're also super absorbent, environmentally friendly, and easy to clean up. They do, however, disintegrate after a few days and can get somewhat dusty— not the best for tiny baby rats.

Sani-chips, which are available in maple as well as aspen, get a high rat rating, too. These small, heat-treated chips are fresh smelling and absorbent. Their only major disadvantage is that, being small and light, they scatter everywhere—though, of course, for aquarium owners this isn't a problem.

Corncob bedding or litter is sometimes used for rats. The regular, untreated brands—such as Andersons, Hagen, Kaytee, or Pestell—can be found almost everywhere. Or try treated Clean-N-Comfy, which has deodorizing enzymes for improved

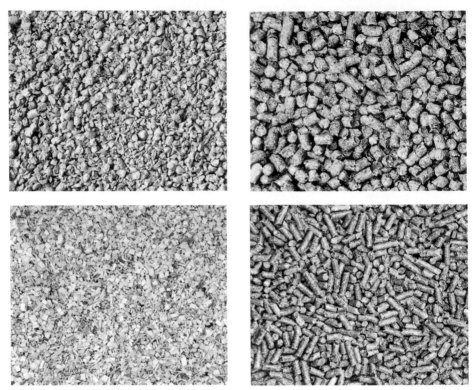

Search out phenol-free wood bedding for superior absorbency and odor control.

odor control. Corncob bedding is inexpensive, and rats love to root through it. It can, however, draw humidity out of aquarium air, especially in the dry winter months, increasing a young rat's chances of getting ringtail. So it's best to use corncob bedding for older rats. Though here again, you have to be careful if your rats are in an aquarium because corncob bedding can become moldy if not changed frequently. When your rats are in a wire cage, keep the Dust Buster handy—you'll need it for corncob cleanup.

Does newspaper make good bedding? Recycled paper pellet products, such as Kitty Soft, Sheppard & Greene, or Yesterday's News, are fine, but your own yesterday's newspaper is not. The paper pellets are fairly absorbent, nontoxic, and don't scatter easily. However, the jury's still out on odor control. You also may want to try a different type of recycled paper product, Cell-Sorb Plus. This shredded pellet bedding, which comes in everyday gray and luxury white, gets good marks for absorbency and odor control. It also gets a

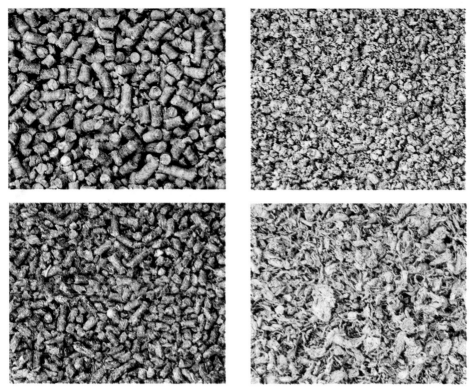

Paper pellets and wood pulp bedding ensure a comfortable ratty home.

higher rat rating for softness and comfort than other paper products.

Your daily newspaper may make economical bedding, but it's not recommended for your rat's cage because the ink rubs off and can be toxic. Do you really want Ratty licking yesterday's headlines off his fur during one of his daily grooming sessions? The newspaper will also stay wet and clammy. Do you really want Ratty lying in a damp bed?

Another possible bedding is nontoxic and biodegradable Care-FRESH. This natural fiber bedding made from reclaimed wood pulp waste looks a bit like shredded egg cartons. You might gripe when the fluff flies out of the cage, but the rats will find it cozy and comfy.

Some of the newer beddings on the market are made from grain by-products and grasses. Two pelleted products to look for are Cat Works (grain) and Critter Country (grass). Both are biodegradable, nontoxic, flushable, and at the high end of odor control and absorption.

Most rats love to curl up in old sweat pants, old jeans legs, old

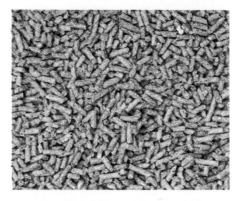

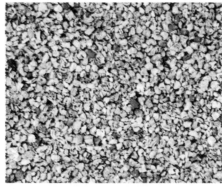

Grain and grass for odor control that lasts

burrow and nest. Try putting a piece of soft material into a corner of the cage for your pet to sleep in, then cover the rest of the floor with the commerical bedding of your choice to soak up any puddles. If you arrange the cage this way, then the sleeping material can be changed frequently, or even daily, so that Ratty always has a fresh place to lay his little head. The rest of the cage can be cleaned out as needed.

Of course, any material that you use will be Swiss-cheesed in no time, so watch that Ratty doesn't get stuck in one of his own chew holes. Watch out, too, for stray threads that could wind around his neck. When in doubt, throw the cloth out. And when there's more hole than cloth, reach for a new piece.

It might take a bit of trial and error before you and Ratty find a bedding that you can agree on. But whatever you choose, remember—*no* untreated pine and *no* cedar.

Nutritional needs

Now that you've picked out cage and bedding, it's time to consider your pet's nutritional needs. Rats aren't picky—they'll eat just about anything, but this doesn't mean you should feed them just about anything. Like you, Ratty needs a good diet if he's to stay fit as a fiddle and alert for training. With this in mind, what should be on Ratty's daily menu?

The choice for his basic nutrition is between lab blocks and small

sweaters, old socks, old towels, old just about anything. Cast offs ready for the rag bag not only keep Ratty warm, they also satisfy his need to

"Did someone say dinner?" Lab blocks and seed mixes meet your rats' basic nutritional needs. Supplement them with fresh fruits and vegetables.

can bet that the blocks will be boycotted every time. What happens if you offer only blocks and they're boycotted? Try a different brand. You might find that your discriminating diner prefers one brand over another.

Whatever you choose for your rat's basic diet, don't run out and buy the biggest bag you can find. Instead, buy a small bag, and store it in an airtight container. This way, when dinnertime rolls around, Ratty will be getting fresh and nutritious food, not stale leftovers.

Be sure to supplement the basics with *small* amounts of table food. Fruits, vegetables, pasta, rice, cooked chicken, and small portions of cheese and nuts are all on the "let

animal seed mixes. Prices are about the same, but in the long run, lab blocks are more economical and nutritious. With seed mixes, the little rats pick out their preferred tidbits and turn up their noses at the rest. With blocks, on the other hand, Ratty can't single out the sunflower seeds. He has no choice but to eat everything, giving him all the nutrients he needs for a balanced diet.

Rats raised on seed mixes might not be too thrilled to wake up one day and find only lab blocks on the menu. Better phase the blocks in gradually—seeds one day, blocks the next. If you offer both together, you

Ooohhh...peaches!

Keep lab blocks off the floor in a wire feeder basket.

'em have it" list. (See Chapter 9 for more information on what's OK and what's not.) Any table foods you offer should be fresh and unblemished. Never give Ratty anything you wouldn't eat yourself, and remove leftovers promptly because spoiled food can be a health hazard.

A diet of lab blocks, supplemented with well-chosen table food, will give Ratty just what he needs—a

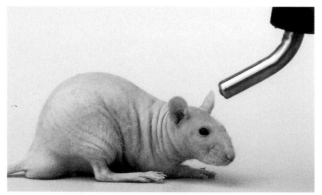

Keep your rat's water clean and fresh—use a sipper bottle.

well-rounded diet, high in fiber, and fairly low in protein and fat.

Place settings

To put it bluntly, rats don't have the most elegant table manners. Not only do they mess *with* their food, they don't think twice about messing *in* their food. So what type of dinnerware does Ratty need to keep his food and water free from pee, poo, and bedding?

For water, the answer's easy—get a sipper bottle. Why? If you put a water bowl on the bottom of the cage, H_2O won't be the only liquid in it—water bowl, toilet bowl, it's all the same to Ratty! And as he plays around the cage, contaminated bedding will also land in the bowl. With a sipper bottle, you don't have these problems. However, even with a sipper bottle, the water will become contaminated every time Ratty touches the ball valve with his tongue or his paws. Good hygiene is a must, so clean and sanitize the bottle every day.

What are the other advantages to sipper bottles? They don't take up floor space, they can't be knocked over and soak bedding, and they're available for both wire cages and (with suction cups) for aquariums. However, you might want to invest in a metal bottle protector so that Ratty can't chew a hole in the bottle and flood his cage. If the sipper drips, return it to the store and try another brand.

Food bowls are a bit more of a problem. Again, an open bowl is an open invitation for Ratty to foul his food. For lab blocks, your best bet is to buy a hopper or a feeder basket. Attach it to the side of the cage or aquarium, and fill it up with lab blocks. Ratty has to nibble at the cubes or work them out one at a time—no longer can he piddle in his dinner bowl or scatter the blocks onto soiled bedding. A plastic feeder basket will have to be replaced every so often when Ratty chews through it, so a wire basket is a much better buy.

Of course, a feeder basket won't work for seed mixes or table food. A good answer, although not a perfect one, is a bin or J-feeder. (Nothing galvanized, please.) Just be careful where you attach it on the side of the cage or aquarium—too low and Ratty will crawl in for a snooze or a bathroom break, too high and Ratty can't get at the food.

Hand feeding is the most direct way to get fruits and vegetables into Ratty, and it's an easy way to avoid contamination. When you're out of time, though, try stuffing carrots, celery, or apple bits into a veggie holder.

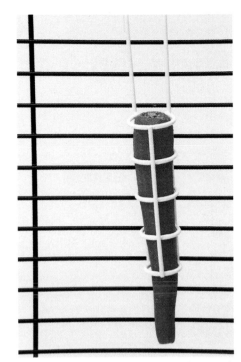

Fresh food and vegetables stay clean and appetizing in a veggie holder.

Vet check

Chances are you won't have to dip into the piggy bank too often for veterinary bills when you own rats. After all, they don't need annual vaccinations, neutering or spaying isn't usually necessary, and medical procedures that are commonplace for larger animals are not always practical for pint-sized pets.

There might be times, however, that your rat does need veterinary care. Check your rat care guide for a list of symptoms to watch for, and try to find a veterinarian who specializes in small caged animals or who knows what's what with rodents. Call around, ask questions. You may not find "Rat Specialist" listed under *Veterinarians* in the Yellow Pages, but some veterinarians know more about rats than others.

Chapter Two
Picking Teacher's Pet

Get picky about your pupils

Everything's ready at home; all you need now is the rat(s). But which rat? From where? What type? What color? Male or female? One or more? Whew—slow down! Take time to do some pre-pet research if you want to pick out the rat that's right for you and right for training.

Finding trainees

Where are you going to find your trainees? For a start, visit your local pet shop and see what's available there. This is where most rat owners buy their pets. No rats in stock at the neighborhood pet mart? Then let your fingers do the walking—call around, find out who has rats, and go take a look.

Another route is to visit a breeder. How can you find out if there's one in your area? You could start by asking the staff at nearby pet shops or veterinary clinics. Better yet, check the Internet or get in touch with the organizations listed at the back of this book.

Shelters are another possibility. Your local humane society or animal shelter may get rats in from time to time. This is more likely in larger cities, but it never hurts to try. If there are no rats available when you phone, put your name on a callback list. One thing to think about if you adopt shelter rats—those raised together should stay together. It's not fair to break up the family.

Whatever route you take—pet store, breeder, or shelter—look beyond the rats. Scrutinize their living conditions, too. Does the facility meet your standards? Are the cages clean? Do the rats have plenty of room? Are they handled and socialized? A rat that comes from a good environment tends to make a happy, healthy pet, and one that's been handled frequently is a good candidate for training because it has already learned to trust humans.

Male or female?

Will it be a big buck or a dainty doe? That is the question. Besides the obvious sex difference, there are other differences to take into consideration. Females are small and sleek, quick and curious. They are half the size of males but twice as mischievous. Keep an eye on them—they like to explore, to get into everything, to steal and hide stuff, and to nibble, nibble, nibble as they go.

Males, on the other hand, are considerably larger than females. Unless neutered, they have a stronger odor, greasier fur, and do more urine marking than the ladies, so they'll need more scrubs in the tub. Male rats are usually laid back and easygoing. They'll happily sit on your lap on Saturday nights. You can be couch potatoes together! Sometimes, however, an intact male rat becomes superhyped on hormones. These Mr. Machos can be aggressive both to humans and to other rats. For horrible-to-handle hormone cases, neutering is often the kindest course, because it reduces the high levels of sexual frustration in the rat and makes it a happier animal. It also makes the rat more docile and trainable. To neuter or not to neuter? There are pros and cons both ways . . . discuss them with your veterinarian.

Does gender make a difference when it comes to training? Because females are quicker and more skittish, it's a good idea to let them play around for a while before training sessions start. However, when they get down to business, they learn quickly because they're so curious. Males, being more lethargic, sometimes have a ho-hum attitude to training, but when they do spring into action, they're more likely to concen-

Is this the right rat for you?

trate on the task at hand without skittering off.

One last word about sex: pick male *or* female, not male *and* female—unless you want to rival the Pied Piper.

A winning personality

Gender is not the only factor to affect trainability. Personality is important, too. Just like the family dog or the ferret next door, each rat is an individual. Some are go-getters, others are lazy. Some are daredevils, others more timid. Some are outgoing, others a little shy. Not all rats of the same gender, or from the same litter for that matter, train with equal ease. But whatever their personality, most rats have very winning ways. They're anxious to please and will give training their best shot.

Class size—
one rat, two rats,
three rats, four?

Is yours to be a one-rat family? Would two be twice as nice? Or, is a rat pack more your style? Costwise and carewise, it doesn't make much difference whether you have one rat or several, and it doesn't make much difference trainingwise, either. If you have one rat, she'll learn quickly because she'll have your undivided attention; if you have several, they'll learn from each other as well as from you.

So why not consider the class size question from the rats' point of view? The fact is, rats like to be with other rats. They like to play together, groom one another, and sleep in a heap. If you're out a lot during the day, an only rat will be a lonely rat, but provide a companion or two, and they'll have no time for singing the lonesome rat blues. Don't worry that you'll be odd man out—they'll treat you just like one of the gang.

Here's something else to think about. Rats are nocturnal animals. Although they'll happily come out to play whenever you're available, nighttime is when they really let their hair down. But how much fun is a party of one? Wouldn't it be better to provide your pet with a rat roommate or two so they can live it up while you're dead to the world?

Multiple rats are the best way to go, but sometimes there isn't any choice. If you vote for five rats and mom declares a one-rat restriction, then you'll have to take on the role of rat pal yourself. Spend extra time with your pet, and give it extra attention. Also, take a good look at Chapter 5, "Learning Through Play: Make the Cage a Playground." It's up to you to see that your single rat has plenty to do when you're not around.

Two's company.

Finnegan is a hairless rat—one of the more exotic breeds.

Plain or fancy

Rats run the gamut from ordinary to exotic, but trainingwise it makes not one bit of difference what you choose. So go ahead and pick out whatever appeals to you. Is an everyday rat just fine? Look for it at your local pet store. Do you have your heart set on something out of the ordinary? You'll probably have to contact a breeder.

Here's a sampling of what's out there ratwise. Commonplace and readily available rats include albino (white with red eyes), hooded (white with colored head and back stripe), and the more common solid and variegated colors like brown, black, and agouti.

Are you in the market for a more unusual rat? Colorwise, look for blue, Siamese, or lilac. Coatwise, check out rex (curly hair) or velvet (velvety

fur). A step above unusual is the definitely exotic such as Manx (tailess), Dumbo (big ears), or hairless (self-explanatory). Confused? No wonder—there's a myriad different rat categories, colors, and hair textures. It takes some research to sort it all out. But the bottom line is, whether you spend a little or a lot, whether you get a rat that's run-of-the-mill or one-of-a-kind, you'll have a super pet that's sure to please.

Also bear in mind that some people are allergic to rat hair, urine, and dander. Are you prone to allergies? Before making rats part of your family, snuggle with some at the pet shop for at least an hour. If you wheeze, sneeze, or itch, those rats need to go to some other family. Don't give up, though. Search out a source of Rex or hairless rats and try the rat handling routine again. Many allergy sufferers who can't tolerate the run-of-the-mill furball rat can often tolerate these specialty breeds. You might be on of the lucky ones!

Selecting students

Now it's decision time—time to pick out your very own rat(s). Faced with a cage full of candidates, how do you know which one(s) to choose? For trainability, you want a rat that's in tip-top shape, physically fit, and mentally alert.

How do you recognize a healthy rat? Look for an active one with bright eyes and shiny coat; with no discharges, no wounds, no bald spots (unless, of course, it's a hair-

The ideal trainee is friendly, curious, and energetic.

A healthy rat has bright eyes and glossy fur.

less); and with absolutely no sneezes or sniffles. Rats are prone to respiratory illnesses that can spread from one rat to another in no time. So even if the rat you're considering isn't sneezing but her sister in the same cage is, go visit the next pet shop.

For training purposes, try to get one that appears friendly and unafraid, energetic and curious. Ideally, you want a young rat that's been handled a lot. Handled rats are already hooked on humans, so bonding will be a breeze. But don't pass up an older rat if your heart's set on her. Rats are apt pupils, and she'll learn to be your best buddy in no time.

Chapter Three

Lessons in Building Trust

Hassle-free homecoming

The great moment has arrived. You've picked out the perfect rats to be part of your family, and you're off to pick them up. It's an exciting time for you, but it can be a frightening time for the ratties. Your job is to make Jack and Jerry's move to their new home as stress free as possible.

The first step is to make them comfortable for the ride home. The salesperson at the pet store will probably plunk the rats into a small, cardboard budgie box. That's not too homey—you can do better than that. If Jack and Jerry are babies and you don't have far to go, a cardboard shoe box, with a handful or two of bedding and an old sweatshirt sleeve tossed in, will be perfect. It won't be perfect, though, if the boys are full grown and you have a long drive home. While you're driving, driving, driving, they'll be chewing, chewing, chewing then running, running, running. So for longer drives home, better buy an inexpensive, small animal carrier . . . and don't forget the bedding.

Whether the trip home is five minutes long or fifty minutes long, resist the temptation to sneak a peek at the new pets, to poke your fingers at them, or to pick them up. They need peace and quiet. Talking of quiet— no ear-splitting music on the radio, please. Instead, talk softly and reassuringly so that bonding begins.

When you reach *your* house, take Jack and Jerry right to *their* house. Gently place them into their cage or aquarium, and then leave them alone. They need time to adjust to their new quarters, time to sniff out their food and water, time to mark their territory, time to arrange their bedding the way they want it to be.

Don't let your kids invite all their friends over to ooh and ahh at the new arrivals. That comes later. For now, the little guys need to settle down and settle in.

Teaching trust

After Jack and Jerry have had time to get their bearings, it's time to work on bonding. Rats seem prepro-grammed to like people, so bonding should be easy. First, you have to teach your rats to trust you, and you don't do this by grabbing them out of the cage. Instead, talk quietly to them and repeat their names softly. "Hello, Jack. How ya doing, Jerry?"

Then slowly open the cage door. Slip your hand in and wait for a rat to come over and investigate. No fast, frightening movements, please. You want them just to sniff you and get used to your smell. After a little while, try petting them gently. If they back away or act frightened, keep your hand still and wait until they come back to sniff again.

What's the next step? It's hand feeding your rats. Choose a choice morsel, such as a Cheerio or a sun-flower seed, and tempt the boys to take it from your hand. Rats love tid-

Tempt your pet with a tasty treat.

Traveling home safely in a small pet carrier.

bits, so it's unlikely they'll be able to resist. If they don't seem interested, perhaps you're offering a ho-hum treat. Try a different one.

The first time you offer food to the ratties, put your whole hand into the cage, hold the morsel between your finger and thumb, and let Jack and Jerry do a grab-and-run. Don't stick food through the cage wires, though. If you make this a habit, Jack could easily mistake your fingers for fast food and nibble or even bite them in his excitement.

When the ratties are accustomed to taking food from your fingers, put a goody onto your flat palm and encourage Jack to climb aboard to get the treat. When he's comfortable with this, you can lift him carefully out of the cage—but never, never, never pick him up by the tail. Cradle him securely in two hands, and keep him close to your body. Jack's more likely to feel safe this way, and you're less likely to drop him. While you're holding him, speak softly and stroke him gently. A few minutes will do, then it's back into the cage for Jack and out of the cage for Jerry. When he's had his share of attention, handling session number one is successfully completed!

The more often, the better

The key to having a sociable, friendly rat is frequent handling. *The more often you handle Jack and Jerry, the better pets they'll be.* This doesn't mean, however, that you have to hold them for hours at a stretch. Several short sessions a day are much better than one marathon session. Are you out all day? Not a problem! Just fit in some handling time first thing in the morning, at lunch time if you're able, as soon as you get home, then again at night. Jack and Jerry will be ready when you are.

Rat on the run

Do you have a rat that wants to run, run, run? Quite a few rats are squirmers and jumpers. Instead of sitting contentedly in your hand, these guys are more interested in running up your arm or trying to

Cradle your rat securely in both hands.

make a quick getaway. Don't panic. This is normal behavior for a healthy rat, and here are some suggestions to help you cope.

Play with him more often every day so he gets to know you. Offer him treats while you're handling him. Sit on the floor during socializing sessions—then if Jack decides to take a dive, at least it won't be a sky dive. Confine your handling to a rat-proofed room (see Chapter 6)—then if Jerry makes a bid for freedom, you won't have to worry. If he does manage to give you the slip, don't go chasing after him. Instead, bring out the treats, and approach him slowly.

I'm the new guy on the block. Anyone want to play?

A family affair

Rats make great family pets. They like people, and they very rarely bite. They'll bond easily with everyone in the family, but you must go about things the right way. And the right way is not the gripe-and-grab method.

"I want to hold him!" Grab, grab.

"No, it's my turn now!" Swipe, swipe.

"No, it's not. I get him next!" Swat, swat.

If this is Jack's introduction to your family, he will *not* be impressed. More likely, he'll be frightened out of his wits.

When it comes to bonding, your rats' best interests should come first.

This means taking things slowly, and teaching the kids to be considerate and caring. Younger children need to be supervised whenever they handle Jack or Jerry. They need to be reminded that rats aren't stuffed animals—don't squeeze, please. Older children should be taught proper handling and care. See the section, "Setting Limits," in Chapter 7.

How to introduce a new rat to the pack

Surprise, surprise! You just popped into the pet store to buy a bag of lab blocks, and you've come home with a new rat, too! Of course you're anxious to open up that cage door and present him to the other boys right away. But wait! You need to give his initiation into the gang some careful thought. Not only do rats need proper introductions to their human buddies, they need proper introductions to other rats.

First off, can you be sure a new rat's 100 percent healthy and not harboring an unsuspected bug? Probably not. So a new arrival should be quarantined in a separate room for two weeks or so. You'll need to buy a small cage for temporary quarters, but don't fret, you'll use it again later. Always wash your hands after touching the newcomer. You don't want any germs hitching a ride to the other rats.

Second, you want to avoid turf wars. The crew in the cage has already established a pecking order and will often gang up on an outsider. How do you prevent the newcomer from being beaten up? How do you help him to become part of the pack?

After the quarantine period, put the new rat's cage next to the main cage—close enough so the rats can see and smell one another but not so close that they can touch (or bite or scratch). Stick to this setup for a few days. Then, it's time for cage swapping. Put the new rat into the main cage and the established gang into the newcomer's cage. This gives all the ratties a chance to get to know one another's smell and to urine mark one another's territory without confrontation.

After two or three cage swappings, it's time for a face-to-face meeting, preferably on neutral territory. The bathtub is ideal (make sure the plug's in) because it's not home to any of the rats and you can separate them easily if they start to fight.

Put the new rat in first to give him the advantage, then introduce one rat from the main cage. Try dabbing each one with vanilla extract to help neutralize their distinctive smells. Be prepared for some scuffling as the rats establish who's boss. The underdog (OK—the underrat) may even flip upside down and start squeaking, "I surrender!" Don't be alarmed. This kind of sparring is normal—just part and parcel of the getting-acquainted process. However, if the rats are really battling big time, you'll have to take action. First, protect your hands with a pair of gloves to avoid being bitten accidentally. Then separate the bully boys by squirting them with water from a spray bottle. Cart them right back to their cages, and give them time to cool their heels before attempting introductions again. In most cases the rats will settle down after a few encounters.

Each rat you already have needs to get together with the new rat. After they've all had their separate introductions, it's time for a group encounter in the tub. Treats all around help to sweeten the meeting. Again, expect scuffling as everyone figures out just where the new guy fits in.

Now, for the final step to successful group living. Clean out the main

I'm king of this cage!

cage thoroughly so it smells like neutral territory. Then pop all the rats in together. It's best to do this during the daytime when they're sleepy and less likely to brawl. If all goes according to plan, the rats will be one big, happy family in no time. If, however, you've bought the rare black sheep rat that's not into community living, you may have to keep him in a separate cage and pay more attention to him yourself. Chances are he'll mellow enough with age and handling to be introduced to the other rats at a later date. Segregation may also be necessary for an intact male rat that becomes particularly aggressive, though in such cases, neutering is often kinder than solitary confinement. If you opt for neutering, be aware that it takes a few weeks after the operation for the rat's behavior to change.

Chapter Four

Tackling that Annoying Gnawing

Nibbling is necessary

Nibble, nibble, gnaw, gnaw—are your ratties chomping and chewing their way through life? Don't take it personally. The rats aren't aiming to annoy you. They're just doing what comes naturally.

Rats need to gnaw to keep their teeth short. Their four front incisors, two on the top and two on the bottom, grow about four to five inches every year. If they don't file down those fangs, they'll look like vampire rats in no time!

You can't teach a rat not to nibble. No matter how often you say, "No, no, no!" little Lola will continue to gnaw, gnaw, gnaw. She doesn't know any better. So rather than going for nibble control, the idea here is to go for damage control.

Material munchers

Watch out first for the shirt on your back. Fabric is a rat favorite. Because rats can munch through material in no time, it's not a great idea to wear your Sunday best when handling your pet. Forget the designer jeans and costly cashmere. It's gardening jeans and tattered T-shirts that the best-dressed rat owner is wearing.

The same goes for the kids. When they're cuddling and cradling the family pet, make sure they're wearing an old shirt, something grungy where another hole won't matter.

Caught in the act.

Watch out if you're sitting in an easy chair with Lola on your lap. That easy chair could be an easy target for rat teeth. There's a simple answer to this problem. Cover the chair with an old bedspread or sheet whenever you and your pet sit down for some prime time.

Have you provided Lola with comfy bedding made from cozy castoffs? Then you'll have to resign yourself to the fact that it will be riddled with holes in no time. When there's more hole than bedding, just raid the rag bag again.

Paper shredders

Besides fabric, another rat favorite is paper. As far as your pet is concerned, any paper within reach is fair game. After all, what better stuff can she find for nesting material? News-

Rats enjoy their own paper supply.

papers, letters, bills, even the kid's homework—if Lola can reach it, Lola will shred it. Just try explaining shredded homework to the teacher!

There's no point in getting upset with your pet when she tears into your term paper. It's not her fault that you left it within rat reach. Be responsible. Keep personal papers safe, and give Lola her own private paper supply.

Whittling away

In their efforts to grind down their teeth, rats will whittle on just about anything. With this in mind, you'll have to think carefully about what goes into the cage. Use metal feeders rather than plastic ones. Be picky, too, about the water bottle. Rats will nibble any edges they can reach. The solution? Go to the pet store, and buy a metal protector for the sipper bottle. Or, place a flat, metal plate, from the electrical supply section in the hardware store, between the bars and the bottle. Or, look for a flat-back sipper bottle without any obvious edges. If your ratties live in an aquarium and they like to hit the bottle, a metal bottle protector will take care of the problem.

Other cage items can also come under attack. The plastic clips that anchor the wire tops of some cages to the plastic bottoms are often a target. They'll need to be replaced every so often. Toys, ladders, and fun stuff won't last forever. Consider these an ongoing expense, and replace them when necessary.

Watch out, too, when Lola is outside the cage for handling and supervised playtime. Never let her out of your sight, or those industrious incisors will make mincemeat of anything in reach.

Tooth-trimming tactics

Your rat is going to chomp and chew whether you like it or not, so it's important to give her something owner approved to whittle on. If you're providing lab blocks as a basic diet, these will give your rat's teeth a good workout. But lab blocks alone won't be too exciting. So, check the pet store shelves for small animal chews such as Kay-Tee wood chews, Super Pet Carrot Chews, Critter Cubes, Swiss Chews, or Nibblettes. Colorful, inexpensive, and non-toxic, these hardwood chews will help keep your pet's teeth trim. Don't, however, be tempted to toss in odd bits of wood leftover from your weekend projects. Scrap wood in your workshop might be treated with chemicals, preservatives, or stains that could be harmful to small animals.

For something different, try Vitakraft Nibble Bars, Nylabone Oodles, regular Nylabones, or small

Rats need to gnaw—give them something to gnaw on.

dog biscuits. Cornstarch-based Booda Velvets are also a big hit with the ratties. They're inexpensive and will keep your rat busy for a while.

You might have to try a few different types of chews to see what tickles Lola's fancy. Keep in mind, though, that just because she's busy chomping on the chewies doesn't mean she'll leave those cage clips alone.

Even if you're a responsible owner and give your pet a wide choice of chews, it's still possible for her incisors to become overgrown. Check her teeth periodically and, if they look too long or excessively curved, it's time to visit the veterinarian. He or she can trim Lola's teeth and/or show you how.

Chapter Five

Learning Through Play: Make the Cage a Playground

Cage time—slack time or quality time?

In the last chapter, you learned that destructive little ratties can be a hazard to your house. In the next chapter, you'll learn that your house can be full of hazards for your rats. Put these facts together, and it's unlikely that you'll want Scamp and Mischief having free roam in your residence. It's also doubtful that you'll have enough hours in your day to entertain the rascals full time. So, unless you're planning to hire a live-in pet nanny, those little ratties are going to spend a considerable amount of time in their cage.

The big question is will this be slack time or quality time? Will the rats be bored to tears, or will they have lots to keep them occupied? Their quality of life is up to you! Scamp and Mischief can't pop down to the store and pick out toys to spice up their life. *You're* the one

who will have to make that cage an exciting place for them. And the more stimulating you make their environment, the more responsive and easily trained they'll be.

Multilevel living

If you paid attention in Chapter 1, you should have purchased the largest cage that you could find and afford. The first step in making that large cage into a challenging environment is to equip it for multilevel living. Rats love to climb, and extra levels increase the living and play areas—more room for fun and games. If your rat's residence already comes furnished with platforms and ladders, that's great. If the platforms are wire, however, cover them with seven-gauge plastic needlepoint canvas to reduce the risk of bumblefoot. This canvas is great because it's easily secured to the platforms with florist wire or paper-covered twist ties, and it allows urine to trickle

A store-bought cage...

... customized.

through the tiny holes instead of puddling on the platforms. Keep the holes free of gunk by giving the canvas a good scrub with an old toothbrush at every cage cleaning.

Is your rats' condo an empty shell? Then it's ripe for renovation! Ready-made shelves can be installed quickly and easily. Super Pet's Corner Look-out Shelf comes packaged with its own ladder. Buy a couple, and arrange them in different corners. Or, Blue Ribbon Pet Products make bird platforms for parakeets that hook onto the cage wires. Buy a few and hang them side by side to make a roomy rat platform. To make them sturdier, use florist wire to tie them together and to the cage.

Not quite a platform—more a tree house or balcony—is a ferret corner

litter pan. Attach one of these high up in the cage. If you buy one with tabs, just hook it over the cage wires. Otherwise, make holes in the pan with a hot nail, and wire or spring hook it to the cage. Throw in some comfy bedding, and watch the ratties hang out.

However, you don't need to go the ready-made route. With a little ingenuity, you can custom make your own platforms. The simplest and easiest way is to have your pet shop special order vinyl-coated metal support brackets from Rolf C. Hagen, Inc. These shelf supports hook onto virtually any wire cage. Then all you need to do is cut a washable shelf to fit between the brackets, and you're in business. For a shelf that's wider than the brackets, double up on the

Flat on the floor or hung high in the cage, a ferret corner litter pan is A-1 for rats.

brackets. In fact, you may want to double up on the brackets anyway so that you can provide Scamp and Mischief with a supersize thirteen-inch-wide platform.

Can't get your hands on the brackets? With a little more work, you can attach the shelf directly to the cage wire. How? Cut the shelf to an exact fit, drill two holes at either end, and attach it to the cage sides with washers and screws.

Or, here's another do-it-yourself platform project to try. Buy some wooden bird perches (flat ones, if possible), line up two or more wherever you want the platform, and Super Glue a piece of washable shelving (Formica, melamine, or Plexiglas) to the perches. What about that scrap cardboard, carpet, or wood you have around the house? Forget it. Any of these will get soggy and stinky in no time.

Now you've made the platforms, but how are the rats going to reach them? You'll have to drill or punch holes through the shelves for bird ladders to hook into. Or, hook the ladders to the cage wires right beside the shelves.

So much for wire cages . . now what are the platform possibilities for aquariums? There are no wires to hang anything on, so free-standing installation is the way to go. If the aquarium is big enough, stacking plastic vegetable bins make good multilevel balconies, and they double as bunk beds at nap time. Add a bird ladder or two for easy entry. You can also make free-standing shelves by

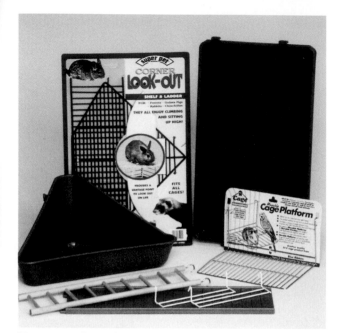

Turn a cage into a home with ladders, shelves, and platforms.

Use a roll-a-nest for a hidey hole inside the cage.

attaching metal corner braces, rigid doorstops, or terra-cotta flowerpots to each end of a washable shelf.

Now that you've put in all this time and effort, will the rats use the platforms and ladders? You betcha! No training needed here. Just give the ratties free rein, and they'll be swarming all over the levels before you can say "Training time!"

Pet store purchases

The multiple levels are installed, the rats have more romp room, now it's time to customize that cage to make it a more interesting environment. The idea is to banish boredom and give Scamp and Mischief new challenges to stimulate those old IQ cells.

A visit to the pet store won't turn up much in the way of rat toys. Don't be discouraged, though. Make a beeline for the bird department, and there you'll find a wide variety of playthings that are just great for rats. Look for hanging parrot toys such as Knot-a-rope or Beak Tweakers. Also look for Comfy perches, bird swings, and arched parakeet ladders. Then stroll by the ferret section for some more great rat toys. Look for ferret balls, giant roll-a-nests, hanging hammocks, and ferret tubes. But skip the hamster tubes—though cute, they're too cramped for rats.

Skip the hamster wheels as well. These aren't big enough for the average-sized rat, they aren't designed to

Kids and rats can both have fun with LEGO.

accommodate long rat tails, and they could injure your buddies. Instead, look for rat-friendly wheels. Plastic Transoniq Wodent Wheels and Fern Manufacturing Sheet Metal Wheels will give Scamp and Mischief a good, safe workout. (See Chapter 10.) Can't find either on the pet store shelves? Then check out both companies on the Internet for ordering information.

Visit the hardware store

Hardware stores also stock rat toys—the clerks just don't know it. Look for PVC pipe or corrugated drainage tube. A foot-long section makes a great rat tunnel. Check out the rope reels, too, because rats love to climb and walk the tightrope. Buy a long length of thick stuff (no sisal, please; it makes the rats sneeze), cut off a good-sized piece, tie knots in it, and hang it from the cage top for climbing. Use the rest to crisscross the cage for high-wire antics.

Before you line up at the checkout, pick up some cheap plastic flowerpots. These make good rat retreats when tied or bolted to the side of the cage. Or, make one into an igloo by turning it upside down and cutting a hole into the side for a door—the wider the pot base the better the igloo.

Everyday items

Not much left in the checking account this month for pet store splurges? Not a problem. A quick look around your own house should turn up everyday household items that can easily be turned into rat toys. For example, take a plastic gallon milk jug and cut good-sized holes in it for an instant play ball. Cut the top and bottom off plastic two-liter pop bottles for instant tunnels (cover any sharp edges with masking tape). To make a hammock, hang up an old dish towel or run two lengths of clothesline through a cut-off jeans leg and tie the clothesline to the cage wires. Or, try suspending a Frisbee from the top of the cage with a hanging lamp chain and hooks. Make a little LEGO house, or toss in an empty shoe box for a place to hide. These are just a few ideas to start you off. Use your own imagination to improvise other toys!

Play school

When the playground's ready, introduce the rats. Scamp and Mischief are going to love their revamped cage, but watch their antics carefully to make sure there are no design flaws in the equipment that could be safety hazards. Keep a close eye on older rats especially. Monitor their play, and modify problem playstuff if they have difficulty climbing or balancing. (See Chapter 14.)

Will the ratties know how to use all the equipment? If you notice that they're ignoring some items, you'll

Rig up a rope in your pets' cage—rats are natural climbers.

Nibble, nibble, nibble—rat toys need to be checked frequently and replaced when necessary.

have to teach them how things work. For example, if Scamp is just sniffing at the running wheel rather than racking up the miles, dot the inside track with little dabs of Nutrical (see Chapter 10) to encourage her to hop

aboard for a whirl. Or, if Mischief's not taking to the tunnels, a trail of cereal bits will encourage her explorations.

When the ratties get tired of the playground setup, change the layout. Move the equipment around, and combine it in different ways to provide new challenges. Or, add a new twist with a new toy. This way, Scamp and Mischief will keep busy and keep their brain boxes working, too.

Replacement costs

The ratties will have a whale of a time with their toys, but this doesn't mean they'll take good care of them. In fact, they'll gnaw through their own stuff just as happily as they'll gnaw through your stuff. So you'll have to resign yourself to inspecting their toys regularly and replacing the unsafe or unrecognizable ones every so often. To keep down costs, don't always spring for those expensive store-bought toys; reuse and recycle household items wherever possible.

Are you grouching about the replacement costs? Then look at things from another point of view. Without the toys, Scamp and Mischief will be bored and lethargic—not the best candidates for training. With the toys, they'll be eager and energetic—enthusiastic students willing to learn.

Chapter Six

Play Place

Out and about?

Does this scene sound familiar? There you go, trotting past the rat cage, saying, "Hi, guys!" They leap up onto the cage wires to greet you, peeping out with their bright eyes, their body language shouting, "Here I am! Come and get me!" What Marco and Polo are really saying in rat language is, "Let me out of here!"

So now you're in a bit of a predicament. On the one hand, you want to play with Marco and Polo, and it's a whole lot easier to let them out to play than it is for you to squeeze into their cage. On the other hand, you've read Chapter 4, haven't you? You know that rats love to chomp, chomp, chomp and chew, chew, chew. So, can you really throw open that cage door and let the little live wires loose?

Some rat owners do allow their rats free roam of the house. For most people, though, this is not a practical option. Think about it. If you let your rats run loose, can you completely guarantee their safety? Can you adequately protect all of your possessions from gnawing damage?

Probably not. However, with *careful* planning and *careful* supervision, it is possible for Marco and Polo to get out-of-the-cage playtime and exercise without harm to themselves or to your house.

Here is the game plan. First, pick a specific area in your house that will be suitable for rat playtime and for training sessions, then rat proof this area completely, and finally, *supervise, supervise, supervise* those rascally ratties.

Picking the play place

Just what area in your house would make a suitable rat playground? What you're looking for is a space that can be closed off from the rest of the house. It shouldn't be too large so it's easy to rat proof. For reasons of hygiene, it should have a washable floor, and there shouldn't be too much (or any) furniture.

Scratching your head over this one, are you? Baffled and bamboozled? It's not as hard to find a place as you might think. How about a bathroom, a laundry room, or a mud room? Whether any of these rooms are a possibility at your house depends on whether or not they can be easily rat-proofed.

Rat proofing

What is rat proofing? It's making the rats' play space safe—safe for them and safe from them. Rat proofing is a matter of looking at a room from a rat's point of view and making sure your rats can't escape or get injured. It's also a matter of preventing Marco and Polo from wreaking havoc as they go about their search-and-destroy missions. Now that you know what rat proofing is, it's time to consider the playroom possibilities in your house.

Bathroom basics

First take a look at the bathroom. In most houses, this is probably the best bet for rat aerobics. Why? A bathroom is usually small, so rat proofing will be less of a hassle. The rats will probably be here for bath time anyway, and it's a practical place for cage cleaning. The ratties could run around a bit while you're looking after their housekeeping. A bathroom is rat friendly, with a washable floor and without much furniture. It's not usually a family-gathering spot. You won't find the family heirlooms here, but you will find a convenient seat!

The first and easiest rat proofing job is just to move the soap, shampoo, and sponges out of rat reach. Marco and Polo won't want to wash with them, they'll try them for treats. Make sure also that toothpaste, hand cream, and make-up are off limits.

Whiirrll!!! Isn't that cute? The ratties are swinging from the end of the toilet paper! Now look! They're yanking it down at top speed. Aren't they precious? You bet—the first time. And maybe even the second time. But rerolling the tissue for the tenth time could be a bit of a pain. So to avoid the bathroom tissue issue, keep the roll out of reach.

If you have a towel thrown over the side of the bathtub or hanging close to the floor on a towel bar, watch out! Your rats will leap up, cling to the towel, and their weight

I'm ready to roam. Have you done the rat-proofing?

Reach for the top!

Anything interesting in here?

will pull it down. To guard against free-falling ratties, move the towels out of rat range.

A bath mat draped *over* the tub is a convenient expressway *into* the tub. Or, your rats might prefer the shower curtain route. Better move the mat and throw the curtains over the rail or fasten them up with a clothespin. Pick up any clothes or towels lying on the floor before your rats reduce them to tatters. Watch the wastebaskets, too. They aren't full of garbage as far as your rats are concerned. They're treasure troves waiting to be looted.

Now that you've picked up whatever is pick-up-able, it's time to scrutinize the plumbing. Wherever there are pipes coming up through the floor or going into the wall (even if they're in a cupboard), check for gaps. Anything larger than one-half inch needs immediate attention before Marco or Polo squeezes through. Plug any hole with wall repair compound. Even small holes need to be patched because the little gnawers will make that half-inch hole into a two-inch hole the minute your back's turned.

Pedestal sinks and their plumbing need to be checked out, too. The back of a pedestal sink isn't solid. There's an opening either high up out of rat reach or low down in rat range. Take care of the openings in the trouble zone with quarter-inch chicken wire. Ball it up, and wedge it in tightly. Unless your sink's in the middle of the room, the wire will never be noticed.

What do you mean I'm not allowed under the sink?

The sink vanity is next on your checklist. Make sure it's flush against the wall. Most vanities don't have a back, so if your rats can squeeze behind, they'll be able to get right into the cupboard. What a field day they'll have then! For a permanent solution, nail on a piece of molding trim wide enough to cover the space. Then carefully inspect the kickboard under the vanity. Any gap between the kickboard and the cupboard is an open invitation for your rats to slither right in. Who knows what escape routes could be under there? Or, Marco and Polo might like this vanity motel so much that you can't get them out when you want them.

How do you board up the gap? For a narrow opening, nail up or glue on a section of quarter-round wood molding or other trim to cover the space. Where there's a large gap, it might be easier to remove the old kickboard. Then either cut a higher one to fit or insert a piece of thin pressboard and nail the old kickboard back on. Don't worry about how it looks. Unless you're lying on the floor, you can't see under there anyway.

Some rats think that the vanity kickboard and bathroom baseboards are put there just to keep their teeth in shape. Great for the teeth—bad for the baseboards! If you catch Marco showing any interest in nibbling these, take prompt action to protect them. What can you try? Your best bet is a piece of stick-on vinyl wall base (also known as vinyl baseboard) or a vinyl baseboard corner cap to cover up the attack zone. These come in different colors and can be cut to size. Or, cut heavy-duty clear plastic carpet runner to fit and tape it on with clear packing tape for an almost invisible job.

Heating-vent covers aren't a problem if they're the louvered type, but decorative ones with fancy cutouts can be another story. If the cutouts are too large, it could be bye-bye Marco. If the cutouts are too sharp, it could be bye-bye Polo. Guard against a lost or injured pet—swap the fancy cover for a louvered one, and swap any wooden ones for metal ones before the rats gnaw them.

What other bathroom hazards are there? Watch out for electrical cords. If nibbled, these can have a shocking, or even fatal, effect on your rat. They must always be kept well out of rat reach. Alternatively, they can be encased in flexible aluminum conduit. Buy it by the foot in the electrical supply section in the hardware store. Even an unplugged cord can pose a threat to your pet if it is dangling down within rat range. When Marco tries to yank, swing, or climb on it—and he certainly will—the shaver, curling iron, or hair dryer on the other end could fall down and bonk him big time.

If you're not sitting on the toilet, close the lid—Polo could jump right in and have an unscheduled bath. If you're not bathing in the tub, drain the water—accidents can happen. Pick up any throw rugs, and stick down any loose linoleum that attracts your pet's destructive attention. And, if you notice your rats lining up to do the limbo under the bathroom door, better attach a sweep to the door or stuff in an old (repeat, old) towel.

Does your bathroom do double duty as a greenhouse? Then watch out for plant attacks. While Marco's digging in the dirt, Polo could be lunching on the leaves. That's not great for the plant, and it's certainly not great for Polo if the leaves are poisonous. Don't take any chances; move the plants.

The last bathroom worry is the family—people popping in and out (runaway rat), people opening doors (whacked rat), people not watching their step (flat rat). Better educate the family to avoid the bathroom during rat playtime.

Other rooms for rat romps?

In most houses and apartments, the bathroom is the best bet for rat romps. However, everybody's house is different. You might have another room that's more suitable. Do you have a basement rec room that's home to a pool table and not much else? Do you have a mud room without furniture but with a washable floor? Have you a laundry room where you can totally block off the washer and dryer?

The bottom line is that you have to use your common sense when picking a play area. Make sure you can rat proof it completely so that the area is safe *for* Marco and Polo, and safe *from* them. Then *supervise, supervise, supervise* each and every time the ratties are out to play.

Out-of-bounds

Most rooms in most houses will be out-of-bounds for rat playtime. For example, living rooms, dining rooms, and family rooms aren't usually practical rat rooms. Why not? One reason is that the acres of upholstered furniture are a magnet for nibbling and nesting. Also, if antique or country furniture is part of the decor, the rats will certainly add a few more distress marks.

Were you thinking of a bedroom as a play room for your rats? Think again. Bedding is a prime target for material munchers. Whether you like your sheets soft and cozy or cool and crisp, your rats will happily chew holes in them and, before you know it—eyelet-trimmed bedding! And what about Grandma's quilt that was two years in the making? It might be hard to pass off those rat holes as moth holes.

Always supervise the ratties when they're out to play.

"Keep out!" should be the catchword for the kitchen where the rats are concerned. Hygiene is the number one priority here. Marco and Polo don't use a litter box, and you won't find them in the bathroom washing their paws. So, to prevent their bacteria from becoming your bacteria, keep rats out of the kitchen. Remember, too, when it's your turn for kitchen duty, always wash your hands if you've been playing with the rats.

Pet playpens

If there isn't a room in your house that's just right for rat playtime and training sessions, here's an idea that might fit the bill. Look in your pet store for a Grrreat Wall, made by Milestone Innovative Products, or check them out on the Internet. A Grrreat Wall is a portable playpen for small animals. It's a long piece of flexible plastic that forms a circular enclosure twenty inches tall when you unroll it and join the overlapping ends together. Set it up on a washable floor, pop in Marco and Polo with their toys, and you have an instant rat playground. Again, be sure to supervise in case you have a super rat that launches a leap for freedom. High jumpers can be kept in place by attaching a Grrreat Wall Topper—a rounded edging that fits on the top of the Grrreat Wall and makes it practically impossible for small animals to get out.

Is the budget a bit tight? No extra cash for a playpen splurge? Don't worry! A homemade rat run can be put together easily and quickly. First, run over to your neighborhood store and beg for some empty cardboard boxes, at least two feet in height. Remove the top and bottom flaps. Then choose one corner of each box, and cut right down the crease line where the sides meet so that the cardboard can be opened out. Lastly, tape two or more boxes together to form a big enclosure.

Does this pen make a good rat play place? Absolutely! Not only can you customize it sizewise for any number of rats (add more boxes), you can also tailor it heightwise for those jumpers (use taller boxes). After you've put it together, place it onto a washable floor, toss in the toys, mix in the rats, and watch the fun. When the ratties are all tuckered out, they can go back into the cage, and the playpen can fold flat for storage.

Don't, however, treat a play pen as unsupervised day care. The little (b)rats could chew through the cardboard or leapfrog to freedom when your back's turned.

Chapter Seven

Step by Step

Stepping out

Through with the rat proofing? Then it's time for Fred and Barnie's first foray to the world beyond the cage. But before you let them loose, it's important to realize that your rats need a bolt hole, a retreat where they can feel safe and secure between explorations. So if their cage isn't located in the play room or if it's too bulky to carry there, provide Fred and Barnie with a small travel cage—preferably one they're familiar with and that contains some of their own stuff.

How to

Now it's time to give your rats a taste of freedom. This is their big moment, not yours. So sit down quietly . . . on the floor if your knees can take it . . . and let Fred and Barnie explore at their own pace.

The first thing they'll do when you open that cage door is to poke their twitching noses out and have a good sniff. They won't be in a hurry to venture out. In fact, they might even whisk back into the cage. Be patient. Curiosity will soon get the better of them, and their noses will lead them out the door to explore. Watch them sidle out, take a quick scurry around, then make a dash for a safe haven—either you or the cage.

This will be the pattern of their explorations—a fast foray into the unknown, followed by a rapid retreat to familiar territory. Here they'll hole up and bolster their confidence before setting out again to expand their horizons.

Where do you fit into all of this? You're still sitting patiently on the

A first tentative step.

43

floor, keeping an eye on Fred and Barnie, making sure that you did an A-1 job of rat-proofing. You're also a sitting security blanket, a lap for Fred to leap onto when he needs reassurance. Why not give him a double dose of reassurance? By doling out the odd treat, you'll soon get the message across that exploring is nothing to be afraid of.

When you've built up his confidence, be careful not to shake it with loud noises or sudden movements. The object here is to train your pet to be a bold Barnie, not a fearful Fred.

This first out-of-cage experience shouldn't be a long one. Ten to fifteen minutes will do just fine. Then increase the playtime daily until you've worked up to one hour per day and more if possible. As the days go by and the ratties get used to their play space, they'll spend less time hiding inside the cage and more time running around outside it. Before long, they'll be marching around, masters of their universe. Then it's time to bring out the toys and to start the training sessions.

Supervision

No matter how sure you are about your rat-proofing skills, *never, never, never* let your rats run around unsupervised. Just because they didn't get into something this week doesn't mean they'll be as well behaved next week. And if the phone rings or the doorbell dings, don't run off and leave Fred and Barnie uncaged and unsupervised, even for a minute. If you do, those rascally little rodents will have a gnawing good time just as soon as your back's turned.

Rats are cautious when venturing out to play for the first time.

Clare loves her rats and knows how to care for them properly.

Setting limits

Fred and Barnie are fast learners. As soon as they've had a taste of freedom, they'll be leaping onto the cage wires asking for more. So now it's decision time. Is it OK for five-year-old Michael to get the rats out? Can he play with them in his bedroom or only in the rat playroom? Does a parent need to be present?

And how about twelve-year-old Clare? She's responsible enough to play with the rats without supervision, but is she allowed to show off Fred and Barnie to her soccer team after practice?

When there are children in the house, set ground rules and stick to them. Young children should always ask permission from a parent before handling the rats, and their playtime with the rats should always be supervised. It's a good idea for young children to sit down on the floor when they get the ratties out because squirmy rats can be easily dropped. Little kids should also wear pants and long-sleeved shirts around the rats so that sharp ratty toenails won't scratch delicate skin. Older, more responsible children can play with their pets unsupervised as long they've been taught proper handling and care. For all ages, exercise crowd control. Fred and Barnie shouldn't be the entertainment for a birthday party, and they should never be handed around when the soccer team is horsing around.

Out and about.

Piddle and poo

Fred and Barnie may enjoy rat romps in the bathroom, but they certainly won't use the facilities. So where will they do their business? Will they go back into their cage when nature calls, or will they just relieve themselves on the floor?

The good news is that rats rarely poop outside their cage. Any little lapse is usually an accident, triggered by fear. The not so good news is that rats are less particular about where they pee. In fact, when they're exploring outside the cage, it's normal for them to mark their territory with tiny drops of urine. Don't blame Barnie for this behavior. He's only doing what comes naturally, and it's not as if he leaves great puddles on the floor. To take care of any piddles and to take care of any health concerns, a quick mop around with a mild disinfectant is all that's needed to restore the floor to it's pristine, pre-rat condition.

Mind your step

Rats are small and quick. If you don't watch your step, they can easily get underfoot. So, for safety's sake, when they're out playing, rules are a must.

Rule #1: No shoes in the playroom; wear only socks or slippers. Then if you do take a false step, the consequences for your rats may not be so serious.

Rule #2: Sit whenever possible. If you're not walking around, you can't possibly flatten Fred.

Rule #3: If you do have to move around in the playroom (filling food bowls, retrieving errant ratties, cleaning the cage), do the soft-shoe shuffle. Slide your feet over the floor instead of walking normally. Rats can't get underfoot if you don't lift up your foot.

Rule #4: Exercise crowd control. Accidents are more likely to happen when there are more people around to make them happen. So limit the number of players in the playroom and make sure they follow the rules.

Rule #5: Keep the door locked when you're playing with the rats. You don't want someone bursting into the bathroom and bonking Barnie with the door. To save Barnie's bacon, teach family members to knock when they need to get in.

Hey! Exploring is fun.

Chapter Eight
Leash Walking

Are you kidding?

Rats on a leash? Who's out to lunch? But wait a minute—at least give the idea a listen. If you aren't into rat proofing, if your home's too elegant to lend itself to rat romps, or if physical limitations make it difficult for you to run after the ratties, then leash walking indoors is one way to give Minnie and Mimi a workout.

Choosing a harness and leash

You'll give the idea a try? First you'll have to find a lightweight harness and leash. No collars, please—Minnie could choke or could give you the slip.

You probably won't find anything labeled "rat harness" at the pet store, but that's OK. A hamster harness will fit most female rats. Another good choice is a small, figure eight kitten harness cut down to size. Or, try a ferret or guinea pig harness if you have a large Larry instead of a mini Mimi.

Most of these harnesses come packaged with a matching leash. If the one you choose doesn't, any lightweight, small-animal leash will work.

Don't put the harness onto your pet until she knows you and trusts you completely. Then, fit it carefully. You want it snug but not so tight that it's squeezing the life out of Mimi. Take your first practice stroll in an enclosed area so that, if you've misjudged the harness fit and Mimi gets loose, she won't get far.

Indoor track

What area in your house will make a good rat track? Will it be a hallway? Will it be a basement? Ideally, what you're looking for is an uncarpeted area without much furniture—preferably one that can be closed off from the rest of the house in case of escape.

What are the do's and don'ts of leash walking? Do set Minnie down on the floor and let her natural curiosity take over. Let her take *you* for a walk. Do guide her gently, or

"Have you found a harness to fit me yet?"

shorten the leash if she's getting too close to forbidden territory. Don't yank on the leash or lift her up by it; you could hurt her. Don't expect her to heel or start and stop on command—she's not a dog. Don't tie a leashed Minnie to the cage or to a doorknob; she'll chew through anything in range, including the leash.

If you're wondering what to do with Mimi while Minnie's on her exercise break, here's a suggestion. It's just as easy to exercise them together on two leashes as it is to walk them one at a time.

Rats enjoy stretching their legs, but some may be a bit timid at first. So, a few minutes exercise is enough for starters. Then, as the days pass, prolong the practices until your rats become leash-walking pros.

Is leash walking safe outdoors?

Now Minnie and Mimi are used to indoor outings, but what about outdoor outings? Are they safe for rats? Although some owners do walk their harness-tested rats in a well-fenced backyard, the answer in most cases should be NO! After all, can you absolutely guarantee your rats' safety outside? Have you got the world's only escape-proof harness? Are there no stalking cats or predatory birds in your neighborhood? In the great outdoors, there are too many accidents waiting to happen to leash-walking ratties. Why take a chance on their safety?

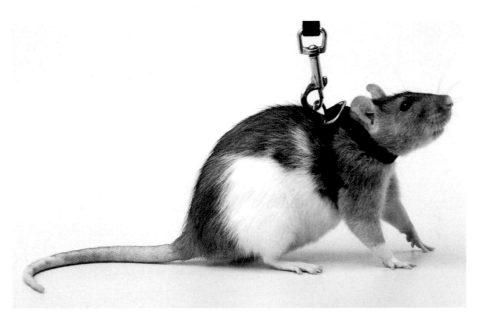

Leash walking in a figure-eight kitten harness.

A whiff of fresh air.

A whiff of fresh air

If out-of-doors leash walking is out for most rats, are there any other ways for Minnie and Mimi to get a whiff of fresh air? On nice days (not too hot and not too cold), why not take the rat cage outside? Put it onto a picnic table or onto the deck, but not directly onto the ground, and make sure it's in the shade because rats are very susceptible to heatstroke. Found the perfect spot? Then sit yourself down, and keep the ratties company. It's very important never, ever to leave Minnie and Mimi alone outside because sneaking cats could come calling, neighborhood kids could get nosy, or the weather could change.

It may be a bit of a hassle to set the rats up outside and sit with them. But when you see how happy they are sniffing the outdoor smells and feeling the soft breezes fanning their fur, you'll be glad you took the trouble.

The rollaround, not the runaround

Are you one of those people who are all thumbs? Would it be a real struggle for you to put the teeny-weeny harness onto the itty-bitty rat? Never fear—Minnie can still get a good workout. Just buy a giant-sized, see-through, rollaround ball. You've seen the smaller ones for hamsters; now you can get super-sized ones for rats. Pop Minnie inside, close the door, and watch that baby roll! But no riding double, please. This is a one-rat ride.

Chapter Nine

Squeaking for Pip-squeak

Calling by name

Rats have been dubbed palm-sized dogs. Does this mean they'll come bounding up to you, tails wagging, tongues lolling every time you call their names? Probably not. More likely, your rat will come right to you when she feels like it, but she won't come when she has something better to do. So, if your voice alone won't always bring her running, what will? A short, sharp sound works better than a voice command to turn Pip-squeak into an obedient little Fido.

To get the lesson rolling, why not take a page out of the psychology books and use the technique of conditioned response?

Conditioned response

What is conditioned response? It's a simple training technique that works well for rats. At a given signal (the stimulus), your rat performs an action (the response), then you give her a reward (the reinforcement). In this chapter, you'll learn how to condition your rat to come running whenever she hears a specific sound.

Rat treats

The key to rat training is finding that to-die-for treat your rat can't resist. The trick is to find one that's good for her, too. Rats are just like you when it comes to junk food— gimme, gimme, gimme! And just like you, they need to say—no way, no way, no way! So lock up the candy and the chocolate, the cookies and the chips, the donuts and the sugary cereals. OK, the odd *tiny* taste of junk food won't pack on the pounds or rot out the teeth, but for the most part, stick to wholesome treats.

Fruits should be a part of your rat's balanced diet. Figure out which one Pip-squeak likes best, and use little pieces for rewards. Will it be strawberries, cherries, grapes, blueberries, banana bits, apple slices, watermelon, cantaloupe, or peaches?

Please squeak again . . . I'd like another one of these.

Veggies also have rat appeal—carrots, corn, lettuce, green beans, peas, tomatoes. Your kids don't like their spinach? Try it out on the rats! How about broccoli and cauliflower? These tumor-fighting vegetables in the cabbage family are particularly good. Wash everything thoroughly before training time.

Other healthy foods you can use as treats include plain popcorn, cooked rice, pasta, crackers, and low-sugar cereals such as Cheerios, Rice Krispies, Puffed Wheat, and spoon-sized Shredded Wheat. Stay away from anything sticky that could make your rat choke, and avoid high-fat foods that cause obesity. However, you can always buy low-fat cheese and no-fat yogurt. They'll be better for Pip-squeak and keep you slim and trim, too. There aren't any low-fat avocados yet, but small tastes won't hurt.

A trip to the pet shop or the pet supply store won't turn up much in the way of rat-specific treats. What you will find are plenty of goodies for hamsters, gerbils, and guinea pigs. Are these treats good for your rat? In moderation, they are fine—yogurt drops are particular favorites. Just be aware that not all small-animal treats appeal to all rats, and you could spend a fortune finding something your rat loves. After all, you can't get samples or return opened bags.

However, returns won't be a problem with the vitamin supplements, Ferretvite and Nutrical. If you want a guaranteed I'll-do-anything-for-this treat, buy one of these products at

"Are these treats for me?"

Healthy treats will have your rat feeling on top of the world.

a generous portion as you get with Ferretvite, but it can still be divided or diluted into a number of training treats. After all, just a little dab'll do ya. A word of warning—*never* exceed the recommended daily dosage and *never* give both Ferretvite and Nutrical on the same day. You don't want to overdose your rat on vitamins.

All of the treats mentioned in this section are good for rats, but which one will have your rat jumping through hoops? That's the one you'll need for training.

the pet shop. Rats love the taste, they'll knock one another over in the rush to get at either, and either product is good for them.

With Ferretvite, you can give one-eighth of a teaspoon per half pound of rat per day. So if you have a half-pound Pip-squeak, stick to the one-eighth teaspoon. However, if you have a one-pound Bruiser, that big boy can enjoy a quarter teaspoon every day. This daily ration can be divided into lots of little dabs for training rewards. Is the allowable amount a bit on the skimpy side for training purposes? Try diluting the daily dose with water to make it stretch further.

With Nutrical, the daily recommended allowance works out to an eighth of a teaspoon per three-quarter pound of rat. This isn't quite such

Shake, rattle, or squeak

When you have the treat(s) lined up, the next step is to settle on the sound that will be music to your rat's ears. A short, sharp, shrill sound works best, so why not try a squeaky

A yogurt treat is hard to beat.

Squeak ... *treat.*

toy? Stop at your local pet store and look for one in the dog or cat department, or just raid the kid's toy box. Because your rat shouldn't be playing with it (nibble, nibble), any type of squeaky toy will do (plastic, rubber, stuffed) as long as it has a loud, high-pitched squeak.

If you yourself can give a good, loud, piercing whistle, that'll work too. Is your own whistle rather wimpy? Try a tin whistle or a referee's whistle instead. You could always ring a bell, toot a horn, rattle a can of treats, or shake a box of cereal. Or, if you have nothing suitable on hand, try clapping your hands or knocking on the floor with your knuckles. It's important to pick one sound and stick with it. Switching will only confuse Pip-squeak.

The gameplan

Don't get going on the gameplan until you and Pip-squeak are best

buddies and she's used to eating from your hand (see Chapter 3). She should be completely comfortable with you and associate you with good things like being held and being fed. Only then is it time to get down to some serious training.

Begin by dividing the treats into small pieces or dabs—for example, one Cheerio can make four rewards. Get Pip-squeak out of her cage, and put her into the play area. Give her plenty of time to snoop around and explore, time to make sure everything's the same today as it was yesterday. When you figure she's finished surveying the scene, get close to her with the treat in one hand and the squeaky toy (or whistle, horn, bell) in the other. Hold out the goody so Pip-squeak can smell it. Then as soon as she runs toward it, *squeak-squeak-squeak,* and give her the treat. And repeat, repeat, repeat.

Practice makes perfect. It's constant repetition that ingrains the behavior. But if you're planning one marathon training session each day, think again. You'll get better results with short, frequent sessions. The reward is crucial, too. When Pip-squeak is learning to come to a squeaky toy, dole out a treat each and every time she answers the squeak. After she masters the behavior, the treats can come at random. For rats, this type of intermittent reinforcement—sometimes a treat, sometimes just a pat on the head—does the best job of ingraining a behavior. However, don't skip the rewards completely. If you do,

Pip-squeak will eventually ignore the squeak.

You could run into a problem if you squeak for your pet in the play-room only when you want to pop her back into the cage. Pip-squeak will soon put two and two together and realize that *squeak*-treat really equals *squeak*-treat-cage. So squeak when you have something good to offer, too—handling time or games to play. This way, you'll ensure that Pip-squeak keeps coming when you call.

Will all rats come on cue? Some will catch on more quickly than others. If yours is a slow learner, be patient. And, if you have an older rat, patience is in order, too. Old rats *can* learn new tricks, it just takes longer. Never, never, never get angry or frustrated. Rather than push it, try again tomorrow. Training time should be enjoyable for everyone.

Rat pack

When Pip-squeak is an only rat, teaching her to answer the squeak is fairly simple. But what do you do if you have a gang of ratties? As soon as they hear the squeak, they'll all come stampeding, clambering over one another, fighting to be first. And when they reach that treat, they certainly won't line up one at a time and patiently wait their turn.

Group training is the easy answer. The strategy is straightforward. Before you begin, have the rewards lined up and ready. Give the sound signal—when you squeak for one, you squeak

When your rat answers the squeak, dole out a treat.

for all—then dole out the treats pronto, making sure you don't miss anybody. The group approach can even help rats with a hearing loss or those on the lower end of the IQ scale. When they see the others running to the squeak, they'll join in the rush.

Lost and found

Teaching your rat to come when called isn't just a cute trick. Accidents can happen. So if Pip-squeak ever gives you the slip and wriggles into a hidey hole—*squeak-squeak!* Or if she hides behind a bookcase—*squeak-squeak!* Or if she races into a room that hasn't been rat-proofed—*squeak-squeak!* Then, when she reappears—treat-treat.

Chapter Ten
Fun and Games

Let's play

Why did you buy a pet? Was it for the pleasures of cage cleaning? Of course not! It's playtime that's the highlight of pet ownership. Playtime equals bonding time, and rats love to play. What's more, Spike and Spunk learn by playing, and they need the stimulation. So get out the toys and get to it.

Borrowed from Bowser, pilfered from Polly

When you're cruising the aisles at the pet store, look at the signs. You'll see "Dog Section," "Bird Section," and "Cat Section." Wait a minute . . . where's the "Rat Section?" Rats are shortchanged when it comes to species-specific toys and accessories. Will you need to leave the store empty-handed? No way! Tabby, Polly, and Bowser all have toys your rats will love.

On the cat racks, you'll find cat racket sacks and crinkle bags. These tunnel-like bags crinkle and crackle as the rats rustle around in them. They also serve as nap sacks for tuckered-out ratties. Then there are play gloves with dangling pom-poms and cat wands that look like fishing poles. These toys will keep your ratties dancing, batting, and chasing— in other words, having tons of fun.

Feeling in the money? Want to splurge on Spike and Spunk? Then spring for a carpeted cat-climbing frame or multilevel scratching post. The rats will get a good workout as Spike chases Spunk up and down and round and round. Just don't part with the big bucks unless you're willing to shampoo the carpet now and again to keep the climber clean.

Now, leave the cat department, and turn the corner to the bird aisle. Although many bird toys are designed for cage use, some can do double duty in the rats' play area. For example, wooden exercise centers for parrots or cockatiels make great free-standing workout centers, provided you can accept the inevitable gnaw damage and the need for periodic scrubbing.

There isn't too much in the bow-wow section for Spike and Spunk to snitch. Most dog toys are just not

Wow! Cat wands . . .

. . . and pom-poms!

suitable for rats—they're oversized and overweight. However, you might try the large-size Rruff Stuff or Booda Bone tug ropes. Hold one end in your hand, step onto the other end with your foot, and let Spunk mountaineer to the top.

It's off to the ferret aisle next for a good selection of rat-sized and rat-suitable toys. Check out the plastic ferret balls with matching tunnels. These are big enough for rats and

stand up well to chew attacks. Large roll-a-nests make great play balls and hidey-holes for the ratties. Pop in a soft cloth and Spike will think he's hit rat heaven. Ferret cloth tunnels and sleep bags are also great for Spunk as long as you figure replacement costs into your budget.

Steer clear of hamster toys, however. They're cute and colorful, but they're too small for rats, and they won't stand up to gnawing.

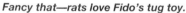
Fancy that—rats love Fido's tug toy.

Homemade fun

Are you budget minded? With a little imagination, you can turn ordinary household items into no-cost rat toys. A few minutes is all it takes to rinse out plastic gallon milk or water jugs and cut holes big enough for Spike and Spunk to run through. Add a new twist by linking several jugs together. How? Cut off the tops and bottoms of two-liter plastic pop bottles, and use these as connecting tunnels between jugs.

Why not add a sandbox to the playground? Pick up a vegetable bin in the kitchenwares section of your local discount store. Pour in two to three inches of potting soil, add a bird ladder for easy access, and watch the little darlings dive right in. Buried treasure, like sunflower seeds or yogurt drop pet treats, will make the adventure more exciting.

Something as simple as a brown paper bag filled with scrunched-up paper gets rave reviews from the rats. To liven things up, throw in a few Ping-Pong balls. Some rats like them, some don't. Or, how about taking Spike and Spunk for a spin in a homemade wagon? Round up two everyday items, a shoe box and a piece of string, attach the string to the shoe box, and voilà—an almost instant ratmobile!

Rat wheels

Did you know that many rats like to spin their wheels? Exercise wheels, that is. Many people don't realize this because they never see rat wheels on the pet store shelves. The only ones usually available are small, eye-catching hamster wheels, and they're positively hazardous to

When the cat's away, the rats will play.

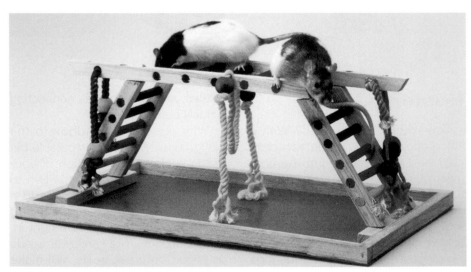

A bird gym doubles as a rat playground.

rats. They're much too small and can seriously injure rat tails. If you can find the right wheel, however, many ratties will take to the track with enthusiasm, especially if they're given the opportunity at a young age.

A running wheel for a rat should be at least 11 inches in diameter, 12 inches is even better, and 15 inches is the best size for a large male. The running surface should be solid so that the rat's tail can't poke through metal rungs or wire mesh and get injured or snapped off.

What kind of wheels are just right for rats? Transoniq Wodent Wheels and Fern Manufacturing Wheels are good examples of what you're looking for. The Wodent Wheels are plastic, while the Fern wheels are powder-coated sheet metal. Both can be used as free-standing units or mounted on the cage, and both are a breeze to clean.

For best results, start your rats wheel running when they're young. If they're reluctant to hit the track, little bits of Rice Krispies or Cheerios stuck around the inside of the wheel with dabs of Nutrical or Ferretvite will encourage them to get those little legs working. As Spike keeps moving from treat to treat, the wheel automatically starts turning, and he starts running. This is how he gets the feel of things. Don't be surprised, though, if Spike loves the wheel and Spunk gives it the cold shoulder—about 20 percent of rats aren't into treadmill running. But for those who are joggers, the wheel provides a great outlet for their energies, especially if the wheel is cage mounted so that the rats can get at it whenever they want. Rats that have wheel access only at playtime are more apt to ignore it because they're too busy exploring other things.

Games

Game time is fun time . . . and it's cheap! Rat wrestling is an all time favorite. The rats already enjoy wrestling with each other. Now it's your turn to get in on the action. If you think Spike's at a disadvantage sizewise, don't worry—you're only going to be using your hand. Pretend your hand is a rat. Dart it back and forth and side to side under Spunk's nose. When he lunges at your hand, move it again. If he does manage to

Join me in a whirl?

Spike enjoys a game of twitch and tug.

with a cotton swab instead. Wave it in front of Spike, and let him bat it back and forth. Be gentle, and don't let the game get out of hand. The aim is to give Spike some sparring practice, not to make him a punching bag.

Twitch and tug is another game that's easily organized and appeals to rats. On the simplest level, all you need for this game is a tissue, a paper towel, or a small scrap of material. Get Spike's attention by waving the tissue in front of his face. Then, as he makes a grab for it, jerk it backward just out of reach. When Spike leaps forward again to pounce on the tissue, tantalize him once more by tweaking it out of rat range. A slightly more sophisticated version of the game involves tying a shoelace to a small ferret chew bone, a wooden chewie, a Cheerio, or a Fruit Loop. Again, it's tugging and twitching the lure out of rat reach that keeps Spike leaping and lunging for more.

jump on board, shake him off gently, and watch him come back for more. Try tussling, too. Take hold of Spike and gently wiggle or tickle him. Call out the word *wrestle* as you play this game. Some rats can learn to connect the name with the game.

Is wrestling not your rats' sport of choice? Then try boxing. Forget the boxing gloves, though—arm yourself

Fishing for treats is a game you have to teach your rats, but, because there are treats involved, they'll be willing students. Go down to your local party supply or cake-decorating store and buy a sleeve of small plastic shot or shooter cups. Tape or paper clip a length of string to one of the cups and pop in a treat. Set Spunk on top of the cage or onto a chair. Tie or tape the loose end of the string close to him, so that the cup dangles down just over the edge of the cage. Then, show Spunk what to do. By pulling on the string, bring up

Peek-a-boo.

the cup within rat reach so that he can grab the treat. Next, put in another treat and, after putting Spunk's paws onto the string, help him to pull it up. With practice, he'll get the hang of things and will soon be able to haul up the treat basket on his own from lower and lower levels.

Rat gymnastics

When it comes to gymnastics, a rat is a natural. Show Spike a rope and he'll shinny up it. Provide Spunk with a bird perch, and he'll patter across it. However, be realistic. Just because rats are great climbers and balancers, don't expect them to do their circus acts on thin ropes or narrow perches. If Spike is going to be rope climbing or tightrope walking, he needs rope three-quarters to one inch thick, and if Spunk is going to be beam balancing, he needs a bird perch broad enough for firm footing. Let him strut his stuff on parrot perches, flat perches, or those made from tree limbs.

It's easy to train your rats to climb a rope. Buy approximately five feet of thick rope, and to keep the ends from fraying, either melt them with a lighted match or wind duct tape around them. If you can't find thick-enough rope, braid three or four lengths of cotton clothesline together. Then loop the rope over a towel bar, and secure it to itself with a piece of duct tape. To keep the rope taut, put your foot onto it, put a heavy weight on it, or tape it to the

floor. Now set the rats next to the rope, and see what they do. Oh, look! Spike has set out to scale the heights. Look again . . . Spunk is staying at base camp. How do you train Spunk to get in on the action? Tempt him up. Put him at the bottom of the rope, hold a treat under his nose, let him sniff it, then slide your hand up a few inches so that he has to stand up against the rope to get the treat. Repeat this a few times. Then raise the treat a little out of reach so that he has to climb up the rope an inch or two to get the goody. After he's mastered this small step,

Up, up, and away.

train Spunk upward and onward an inch at a time. He'll reach the towel bar summit in no time. But how's he going to get down? Some rats slither down head first, others slide down tail first, some won't come down at all. If you've got a scaredy-rat stuck at the top of Mount Towel Bar, scoop him up and airlift him to safety.

Most ratties are adept at high-wire walking. Again, thick rope is the secret to success. Although you'll probably want to provide ropes inside the cage, that's not the place to begin tightrope training. It's better to begin by stretching rope between two chairs, a start chair and a finish chair. Tie or tape the rope taut, and lay plump pillows on the floor underneath as a safety net. Don't put Spike on the start chair and expect him to run across the rope to the finish chair. Instead, start things backward. Put him on the rope, a few inches from the finish chair, and entice him toward it. Repeat this a few times until he's got the hang of it. Then, a little at a time, back up his starting point on the rope until even-

tually he's setting out from the start chair. Don't rush this, and never force your rat to do any tricks he seems afraid of doing. If one of your rats is a more enthusiastic gymnast than the rest, teach him first—the others will often follow the leader.

When the rats are proficient performers on the tightrope, crisscross their cage with ropes, perches, and thick branches. Spike and Spunk will have a high old time on these aerial walkways.

When their paws touch ground again, why not teach them how to hop through hoops? An embroidery hoop is ideal for this trick. Start by holding the hoop upright, with the bottom edge touching the ground. Saying, "Jump!" use a treat to entice Spike through the ring. (Of course, he won't be jumping yet, but that's the goal.) As soon as he's comfortable walking through the hoop, raise it up little by little until he has to hop to get through it. Be sure to lavish praise on your hoop hopper—he's added one more trick to his repertoire.

Rats are naturals at tightrope walking.

Brainteasers

Not only will your rats enjoy physical activities like gymnastics, they'll also get a kick out of learning games that test their intelligence. Spot the shape, for example, is a good IQ booster. In this game, you teach your rats to pick one shape out of a lineup of shapes. Here's how. Place three or more identical shoe boxes in a row, remove the lids, and cut a door shape in one end of each box. Cut paper flaps to fit the doors and draw or paste a different shape onto each flap—for example, a square, a circle, and a triangle. Finally, tape the flaps to the doorways, making sure they fit and hinge for easy entries and exits.

When the boxes are ready, decide which shape you want Spunk to recognize. Is it the circle? Is it the square? Or is it the triangle? OK, the triangle wins. Although the eventual goal is to get Spunk to go through the triangle flap and into the box, you can't do this in one easy step. Instead, you do it by shaping his behavior a little at a time, using repetition and reward to reinforce the behavior at each stage of the game.

Before training begins, select a sound that will get your rat's attention. Just make sure it's not the same sound you used in Chapter 9 to get your rats to come when called. Snapping your fingers or ringing a bell will do nicely. Made your choice? Now start the shaping process.

• Put a tiny treat in front of the door that has the triangle on it.

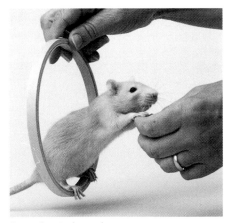

Learning to hoop hop.

• Plunk Spunk a couple of inches away from the treat.
• Let him go so that he makes a bee-line for the food.
• When he grabs the goody, ring the bell.
• Repeat, repeat, repeat.

At this point, Spunk should associate the sound of the bell with getting a reward. If he isn't cooperating, either he's not hungry or you have the wrong goody. Switch treats, or try again later.

OK, your rat's hitting that treat 100 percent of the time. What's the next step?
• Put the treat in front of the door again.
• Move Spunk an inch farther back from his previous starting point.
• Let him go, and ring the bell when he gets the goody.
• Repeat, repeat, repeat.

Now comes the tricky part because you've got to do two things at once. Keep shaping Spunk's progress an inch at a time until eventually he's sprinting two or three feet to reach the treat at the triangle. At the same time, start ringing the bell before Spunk reaches the reward. Then ring when he's a little farther back and a little farther back from the treat. Why? You do this so that Spunk associates the bell ringing with going for the reward, not with grabbing it. Eventually, the bell ringing will be the signal for Spunk to start his sprint to the triangle. You'll have to practice this routine over several days or weeks, but persevere—in next to no time it will be ding-dash-dine.

So now Spunk's getting *to* the door, how do you get him *through* the door? That's easy, keep shaping. Put that treat right in the doorway, half inside and half outside. Next, have just a smidgen of treat showing under the flap. Finally, put the whole treat behind the flap.

When he's going through the triangle flap consistently whenever you ring the bell, it's time to make sure it's the shape he's learned and not the position of the box. Shuffle the boxes around. See if he goes to where the triangle *is* or to where the triangle *was*. If he hits the triangle—congratulations! If not, it's time to shape his behavior again.

Can you teach your rodent student to recognize the circle and square, too? Why not give it a try when he's passed the triangle test? Just make sure to use a different sound for each different shape.

Chapter Eleven

A-Maze-Ing

One smart cookie

Rats may be small in size, but they're big on smarts. If you want to see for yourself just how smart your pets are, why not teach them to run a maze? Mazes will keep your rats on their toes, give them something fun to do, and challenge their intelligence. Making mazes will challenge your intelligence and get the whole family in on the action.

Back to the pet store

Where are you going to find a maze for Frisk and Frolic to run? You won't find a prepackaged rat maze at the pet store, so you'll have to improvise. If you're short of time but not of cash, colorful, hard-plastic ferret tubes, tees, elbows, and balls can be quickly snapped together in a variety of ways to make simple or complex mazes. These see-through tunnels make maze running a spectator sport—you can watch your rats' progress as they maneuver through the course.

Start small with a few basic sections. When Frisk and Frolic have mastered this minimaze, make it more complex. Add extra sections, change the layout, and introduce a dead end or two. Dead ends can be rigged up easily. Either purchase ready-made end caps, or fit a circle of stiff cardboard over the end of a tube section and hold it in place with a collar.

When hunting for ferret tunnels, don't be talked into the flimsier, flexible, accordion type—your rats will chew through them in no time. And, whatever you do, don't substitute hamster tunnels—they're not sized for rats or safe for rats.

Back to the hardware store

If two ferret tubes are all your budget can stand, there is a cheaper alternative. March off down to the building supply store. Ask for black plastic corrugated drainage tubing, four inches in diameter, and have it cut into one-foot sections. Throw in some elbows, tees, Ys, and end

Snap together ferret balls and tunnels for a ready-made rat maze.

caps, then enjoy an afternoon of family fun putting it all together. The drawback to corrugated tubing is that it's not see-through; you won't be able to chart Frisk and Frolic's progress through the maze. In fact, after they've popped into the mouth of the maze and vanished from view, you won't have any idea where they are or what they're up to. So don't start with a monster maze. Instead, start small, and add on one section at a time.

If you can't lay your hands on corrugated drainage pipe, look instead for four-inch-wide PVC plumbing pipe. This tubing comes in ten-foot lengths, so you'll need a hacksaw and some elbow grease to cut it into sections. Don't forget to pick up some tees, end caps, and elbows.

Although PVC is more expensive, it is thicker and more gnaw proof.

Traditional mazes

Are tubes and pipes not your idea of a real maze? With a bit of planning, a bit of effort, a big lidless cardboard box, extra cardboard, and some packing tape, you can manufacture a more conventional maze in an afternoon. The first step is to sit down with a piece of paper and draw up a master plan. Plot the best locations for the entrance and exit. Figure out how many passageways and dead ends you want and where to put them. Then get busy with the scissors. Cut the extra cardboard into the required lengths for the corridor walls, and tape them to the inside of the box according to the master plan. If the box walls are too low and your ratties are escape artists, cover the maze with chicken wire for a see-through ceiling. With a homemade maze, you can watch all the stop-and-go action, and you can intervene if Frisk gets totally lost or Frolic lies down for a snooze.

Are you getting hooked on maze building? If so, check the Internet. Several web sites illustrate more complex maze setups to challenge both you and your rats.

Rainy-day maze

Making a maze doesn't have to be a serious undertaking. Take a rainy day, a few bored kids, and a stressed-out parent. Add some empty cereal boxes, shoe boxes, tissue boxes, and two-liter plastic pop bottles with the ends cut off. Throw in some tape and scissors, and let the kids go to it while you put your feet up. You'll be amazed what they come up with.

For a cheap alternative, plastic drainage pipe fits together easily.

Wait a minute, though! The one problem with a shoe box maze is that shoe boxes don't come with windows. So before the master builders

Shoe boxes + cardboard tubes = a rainy-day maze.

"Did I beat my record?"

get started, help them to make cutouts in the box tops for rat watching. Cover these little windows with clear plastic wrap taped in place.

Training and testing the maze runners

It would be easy to train Frisk and Frolic to navigate the maze by laying a treat trail through it . . . but, that's the easy way out. Any rat can follow a food trail. A much better plan is to let the ratties use their intelligence to figure things out for themselves. This will take trial and error, but it will keep the girls busy and give their synapses a workout.

While the ratties are searching for the exit, you can get busy recording the time trials. How long did it take Frisk to find the exit? Was Frolic's attempt better or worse? Which rat holds the household record for the fastest time? How about the slowest time? Do the girls get faster or slower with age? Will a new rat in the pack follow a maze runner and learn the course quickly?

Keep things lighthearted—maze running should be fun for the rats. Don't make them run if they don't want to, and don't shove them in when they've had enough. It should be fun for you, too. This chapter is for the kids and for those who are still kids at heart.

Chapter Twelve

A Hat-Trick of Rat Tricks

Where's the treat?

Rats are real people pleasers. They're always ready for action, and they're fast learners. Here are three tricks your rats can master in double-quick time—at least they can if you bribe them. It's the old conditioned-response story again—trick-treat, trick-treat, trick-treat. As you learned in Chapter 9, treats are the key to getting your rats to do what you want. So get out the goodies and get going!

Pretty please

Got the video camera rolling? Trying to get some footage of the little darlings? They're not cooperating? Never mind telling them, "Say cheese!" Instead, grab a piece of cheese, and you'll soon have them smiling for the camera. Well, maybe not smiling, but sitting up looking pretty anyway.

Start by putting the rats' cage into their playroom, and let them out and about to run off their energy.

Then, when they've explored to their heart's content, keep one out and put the others back into the cage. It's better to teach this trick one rat at a time, or they'll be leapfrogging over each other to get at the reward.

Take that tiny piece of cheese, and hold it tight. Or, get out the Nutrical or Ferretvite, and squeeze a dab onto a plastic spoon. Hold the spoon close to Scamp's nose until he sniffs the treat. Then while saying, "Sit, Scamp!" raise the spoon up so he follows it. As soon as he's sitting pretty, give him the goody. Then repeat the process. Repetition and reward is the name of the game. Of course, he'll never learn to sit on command like a dog. It's not the "Sit, Scamp!" that registers with him—it's raising the treat in front of his nose that does the trick.

Scamp won't take long to perfect this performance. Your other rats, watching with whiskers twitching, will be anxious for their turn. So put Scamp back into the cage, and bring out Rascal. Since the smell of Nutrical or Ferretvite is in the air, Rascal

Sitting pretty.

will be more than happy to give the trick his best shot.

Soon you'll have all the little beggars sitting up to beg. Can this trick be tried when they're all out to play? Or, is it strictly a one-rat routine? If you use the Nutrical on a spoon as the treat, chances are every rat in the room will be fighting for the spoon. However, if you use Cheerios or Rice Krispies as rewards, then each rat can sit up, get a goody, and run off to eat it, leaving the floor clear for the next rat to show off. Of course, if you're really ambitious and want a doubles act, try a treat in each hand.

What if you have a rat who doesn't want to sit but wants to stand up and be counted? If the goody's good enough, Rascal might bypass the sitting stage altogether and go straight to a stand. That's OK, too, because rats looks so picture perfect when they're standing.

As long as your Rascal's standing, why not take things a step further and coax him to walk along or hop along on his hind legs? Hold a treat under his nose, and lead him along by gradually moving the treat away from him.

Perching pretty

Riding around on your shoulder is a fun way for your rat to see the world. Most rats can master this mode of transportation easily and quickly, but before you issue a ticket to ride, here's what to do.

Get out the veggies and one of the rats. Start by sitting on the floor or on a chair so your pet won't be too high up. Put Scamp on your shoulder, stroke him, and sweet-talk him—in general, make that shoulder a nice place to be. If, despite your best efforts, Scamp would rather run than ride, it's bribery time! Dole out little carrot chunks to encourage him to stay put.

Short practices—a few minutes at a time—are best for starters. As Scamp gets comfortable with his perch, space out the rewards so he'll shoulder sit longer. When you've both got the hang of things, it's time for you to stand up and see if your rat's got a good head for heights. Some rats are laid back shoulder sitters, quietly going along for the ride.

Others are more like fidgety kids who never sit still. They'll pitter-patter from one shoulder to the other, checking out the view.

Even when Scamp's a seasoned shoulder sitter, beware of going into non-rat-proofed rooms. Your hitch-hiker could jump ship at any time, race down your back, and scoot into the nearest hidey-hole.

Pickpocket

Do you have a little ratty who's not inclined to roost? Don't force the issue. Instead, why not let Rascal ride around in a shirt pocket, a sweatshirt pouch, or a jacket hood? Just don't try cramming an oversized Rascal into an undersized pocket.

How do you persuade Rascal to stay put in the pocket and feel at home in the hood? Slip him a bit of fruit from time to time. Getting him to stay there probably won't be your biggest problem anyway—remember the lessons learned in Chapter 4, and make sure your rat's not nibbling holes in your hood while he's holing up in it.

No rat-sized pockets in your wardrobe? Why not opt for a roomy fanny pack? These come in a larger range of sizes than shirt pockets do. A large one is your best bet—Rascal is less likely to fall out or climb out—and a large one lets Scamp come along for the ride, too. Lay the fanny pack onto the playroom floor, and put a few Rice Krispies inside. A folded-up paper towel can be tossed in, too,

to soak up any piddles. Then let your pets explore the pack at their own pace and get familiar with it before popping them in. Always wear the pack on your front where you can watch for bailouts, and leave the zipper partway open so that your passengers won't suffocate.

Standing up . . . the trick is in the treat.

Is your rat a pocket pet?

force the issue. You want this to be fun for them, not frightening. One last point: if the fanny pack starts looking a bit tattered and holey, don't take chances—toss it out and buy a new one.

Anything else?

Are there any other tricks up Scamp's sleeve? There certainly are. Rats can be taught all sorts of things as long as you remember the repetition and reward. Even an old rat can learn new tricks. If you can dream it up, your rat will give it a try. Of course, be practical . . . no fetching the newspaper or barking on command.

Start with short rides, and work up gradually to longer ones. If you drop in a tasty morsel now and again, you can train your pets to stay put. Are your rats reluctant to be fanny pack rats? Again, don't

Teaching your rats tricks is not just a gimmick to make them look cute. Tricks alleviate boredom. Scamp and Rascal will enjoy the stimulation and the challenge. Best of all, it's a great way to help you bond with your buddies.

Checking out the fanny pack.

Chapter Thirteen
The Traveling Rat

Ticket, please

Your rat will be happy to travel with you anywhere you go, but it may not always be feasible for Gulliver to go with you. For example, do you use public transport to get around town? Are you planning to take Gulliver with you on bus, train, streetcar, or subway? If so, be sure to phone the transit company ahead of time and ask if pets are allowed to ride. Some companies will say "No way!" to pet travelers. Others will OK the idea as long as Gulliver is suitably confined. Did Ms. Jones on the phone tell you "Yes"? Ask her to put it in writing. A letter, fax, or e-mail in hand will save potential headaches and hassles when you show up with Gulliver at the ticket booth.

Got Gulliver's ticket to ride? Put him into a small travel cage, and put the cage into a roomy gym bag. This way, your pet will be out of the public eye, he won't panic any passengers, and he'll avoid undue stress and strain on the journey.

If public transport doesn't pan out but your rat has an appointment with the veterinarian, what can you do? Try taking a taxi instead. In fact, you

might want to go this route regardless—two in a taxi equals less stress than the noise, the hustle, and the bustle of public transit. You may have to phone around to find a cab company that will let the meter run for a rat. Show your appreciation—don't forget the tip.

Or, you could always call in a favor from a car-owning friend or acquaintance. Offer to pay for the gas, then sit back and enjoy your chauffeur-driven ride.

The high flier

Most rats will never rack up any air miles. But what if you and Gulliver live in a college dorm and fly home for the holidays? What if you're a senior who spends summers in New Jersey and winters in New Mexico? Or, what if you're getting transferred from Boston to Boise? Then Gulliver will have to get ready for takeoff. However, before he flies the friendly skies, you'll have to do some research.

Different airlines have different regulations about animal travel. Phone the airlines directly with a list of questions. Are rats allowed? At

Does your ratty have a ticket to ride?

what cost? Will that be cabin class with you or cargo class with the luggage? In fact, if you're told *no rats allowed,* ask to speak to the cargo department anyway—you may get a different answer.

When Gulliver's going cargo class, here's something to think about. Although the temperature in the plane's cargo hold is animal friendly, the temperature on the tarmac may not be. If it's 20 below zero when Gulliver leaves Idaho, his fur coat won't be warm enough for the ride from terminal to plane. And, if it's 100 degrees when he's unloaded in Arizona, he can't fling off his fur and switch to shorts.

Whatever way your ratty is flying, you'll have to ask about travel carriers—what are the specific guidelines? Then follow the guidelines to the letter. Talking about letters, get all information in writing well before your departure date. The frazzled employee at the check-in counter may have a different opinion about Gulliver's travels than that pleasant person you spoke to on the phone. You don't want Gulliver grounded, do you?

Whether your rat's going cabin class or cargo class, you'll have to make his travel carrier a home away from home for the trip. Put in cozy bedding, plenty of food, and a mini sipper bottle. It's also a good idea to lock the cage door—padlock preferred—to prevent any accidental or unauthorized opening. Just don't leave the key at home on the kitchen table!

One last point—if Gulliver's part of your carry-on baggage, don't advertise the fact. A rat isn't everybody's idea of the ideal traveling companion. So be considerate to your fellow passengers and keep your rat(s) out of the limelight.

Auto outings

A rat is one of the easiest pets to transport by car—no barking or screeching in the back seat, no inconvenient pit stops, no exercise breaks. Moreover, car outings are a whole lot easier to arrange than public transit—after all, it's your space, you make the rules. And rule number one should be—never, ever let your rat run loose in the car or van. Just picture all the nooks and crannies in a car: under the seats, between the seats, behind the ashtray, beneath the dash. A roving ratty could take a nose dive into who-knows-where for who-knows-how-long. So free roam is out, and travel carriers are in.

For short car trips, like visits to the veterinarian or to grandma's, a small travel cage is all that's needed. Take along a few lab blocks and a container of water for snacking and sipping on the way. A word of advice, however; take the sipper bottle out when the car's in motion. Otherwise, the bottle could jiggle and leak. Even worse, a direct pothole hit while Gulliver's in mid-sip could result in cracked teeth.

For longer journeys, don't coop Gulliver up in the cramped quarters of a tiny cage. Give him "roam-room" in his own cage if it fits into your vehicle, or spring for a large travel cage. Lay on all the comforts of home—food, bedding, chew toys, play tubes—and stop at regular intervals to wet Gulliver's whistle.

Just because you've confined Gulliver to a cage while traveling doesn't mean he won't be getting into things. While your eyes are on the road, Gulliver's teeth could be tackling the seats, the seat belts, or the clothes on the kid next to him. So wherever the cage leans against the seat, shield the fabric from rat attacks. Try slotting an old tray, a leftover piece of plywood, a length of plastic carpet runner, or a flattened cardboard box between seat and cage. Avoid severed seat belts by tucking them well out of rat reach,

For safe car journeys, keep your rat confined.

Bring toys along for the trip.

and avoid trashed T-shirts by having the backseat passengers sit out of rat range.

Whether Gulliver's going on a short trip or a long haul, in a small carrier or in a large cage, don't just grab him and run. He needs to feel comfortable with both cage and car before setting off on any travels. Let him investigate the carrier at playtime and mark it as his own, then go for a few trial rides around the block to get him used to the car. A little time and effort on your part will help make Gulliver's travels happy ones.

Temperature alert

When the mercury's rising or the temperature's dropping, keep a weather eye out for Gulliver. His travels won't be safe or pleasant if he's roasting or freezing. In fact, his life could be in danger if you're not careful.

So when there's a chill in the air, warm up the car, and stuff extra blankies into the carrier. Or, if the sun's beating through the car window, cool the car down before popping Gulliver in. Roll down the windows, or crank up the air conditioner for a while. For your pet, heat is more life threatening than cold—heatstroke can quickly be fateful. Unless your vehicle has air-conditioning, don't travel with your rat when the weather's hot—it's too risky.

If, however, an emergency trip to the veterinarian is necessary, keep Gulliver cool with ice packs wrapped in towels. Use hard-sided packs only, not soft-sided gel bags (chew, chew). No ice packs in the freezer? Plastic pop bottles, partially filled with water and frozen, or margarine containers filled with ice cubes will do in a pinch. Another good idea to keep your ratty cool is to use made-for-baby car sunshades. These attach to the window with suction cups and can be rolled up or down as needed. They can also be moved from window to window to block the direct rays of the sun.

Never, ever leave your pet rat unattended in the car. Remember, hot cars can kill. Even if the temperature outside feels cool, inside the car your rat could be sweltering from the greenhouse effect of all that glass.

Pack rat

Vacation time again? Is Gulliver going along for the ride? Then don't forget to pack his suitcase while you're seeing to your own. Here's a list of travel essentials for the rat that takes to the road:
• food for the trip in a Zip-Lock bag
• bedding

Packed and ready for the road.

• a supply of disposable sleep cloths
• tweezers, spoon, or small scoop for cage cleanup
• Ferretvite or Nutrical
• treats
• harness and leash
• toys
• a supply of plastic bags for waste disposal
• cage cleaner and deodorizer

Pack these supplies into a plastic storage box, a gym bag, a diaper bag, or even a shoe box. If there's room in the trunk, throw in the Grrreat Wall (Chapter 6) . . . and your rat's ready to go.

Hotel etiquette

When a hotel/motel stay is in your vacation plans and Gulliver's one of the travel party, the best advice is to book ahead. Your best buddy might not be welcome everywhere. Even if the motel listing states "small pets allowed," the management might mean "small dogs and cats allowed." So be up-front when you make reservations, and tell them it's a rat you're bringing. Otherwise, if you show up with a rat when the management expected a cat, you could find yourself marooned at midnight with no room at the inn.

When you've found an establishment that's rat-friendly, the first rule of hotel etiquette is the same as the first rule of car travel—never let that rat run loose. He'll find escape routes you can't see . . . guaranteed! This is why you packed the leash and the Grrreat Wall. Just slip on the harness and leash or set up the playpen, and Gulliver can get his exercise safely—but only in the bathroom, please. Any urine and feces can be cleaned up easily, and the floor itself can be wiped up with the cage deodorizer you brought along. This way you'll leave nothing behind but a good impression. At least you will if you keep the towels and shower curtain out of rat reach!

A bathroom is a great multipurpose rat room. Not only can Gulliver use it as an exercise room, he can use it as a bedroom at night. This way when it's 3:00 A.M. and he's swinging from the cage wires, rustling through his bedding, or chowing down his food, he won't disturb your beauty sleep. If, however, you're a light sleeper and Gulliver's a rowdy partyer, maybe you'd better pack a pair of earplugs, too.

Although it's not the best plan to leave your rat alone in the hotel room, if you do have to step out for a while, padlock the cage door. It's always better to be safe than sorry. Also be courteous and leave a large note in a prominent place for the housekeeping staff. It's polite to let them know that there are rats in residence because rats aren't your typical take-along pets.

Ask first

Hotels and motels can say *yea* or *nay* to your ratty. Give your friends and relatives the same option. Just because you rave about your rat doesn't mean that cousin Karl will roll out the welcome mat. So never take Gulliver along uninvited. If you do, the visit could be a lot shorter than you'd anticipated.

Options for the stay-at-home rat

Although Gulliver might be happy enough to tag along on your travels, it may not always be feasible to take him with you. Are you going on a cruise? Sorry, no pets allowed. Planning a city trip for shows, shopping, dining, and museums? It isn't fair for a pet to be cooped up day and night in a hotel room while you're out on the town. Are you planning to go camping, but the temperature's 101 degrees? It's much too hot for rats.

The fact is, sometimes it's better to leave your pet at home in his own familiar surroundings. So for all the Gullivers being left behind, what are the options? First, look at the possibilities for leaving him in your own home. If you're gone for just a weekend and you can set the thermostat to guarantee your pet's comfort, why not let Gulliver pet-sit himself? Load the feeder with lab blocks, hang up an extra sipper bottle, toss in a treat or two, and leave him to enjoy a weekend of rest and relaxation.

However, for anything longer than a couple of days, you'll have to make other arrangements. Got a relative, friend, or neighbor who owes you big time? Looking in on Gulliver once a day shouldn't strain the friendship. Or ask a neighbor kid to take care of your pal. If you're new in town and don't know a soul, a pet-sitter could be the answer.

Sometimes it's more convenient and less lonesome for Gulliver to board elsewhere when you're gone. Maybe that accommodating relative, friend, or neighbor could be persuaded to offer him a home away from home. Or maybe a pet store, veterinary clinic, or kennel in your area will have a spot for him.

Hanging out at home is often the best way to go.

Whatever arrangements you make, be sure to leave the temporary caregiver a list of all the important things—food requirements, your vacation phone number, the veterinarian's phone number, emergency instructions, and anything else you think important.

Chapter Fourteen

Training Tips and Handy Hints

Rats and other pets

Can you train rats to get along with other pets? With smaller animals such as mice, hamsters, and gerbils, it's not a good idea. Rats are aggressive toward smaller rodents, and when the fur flies, you can bet the tiny guy will be the loser. So keep rats and small rodents well apart in separate quarters—never the twain shall meet.

Believe it or not, rats get along better with large pets than with small pets. Ever imagined a runty little rat cozying up to a protective pooch or an inquisitive rat going nose to nose with an aloof cat? It happens!

But is it a good idea? Is it something you should try? It's important to know that there's a real risk to your rat when you play matchmaker. Friendly fraternizing between dogs, cats, and rats is the exception rather than the rule. Why take a chance with your rat's life?

Ferret fanciers, be absolutely certain that your ferret has no access to the rats, even if the rats are caged. Pet ferrets can terrorize the ratties through the cage bars. Worse yet, they can open cage doors and help themselves to an inmate. Bird lovers, keep your feathered friends and your furry friends well apart. Big birds prey on rats, and rats prey on small birds.

Don't risk a mismatch with a pet of a different species. If you want your rat to have a companion, it's better to play it safe and make it a rat companion.

Training changes for elderly rats

Just like people, rats get frailer and less active in old age. Their eyesight, hearing, and agility start to diminish, and they spend more time just sitting around. Gone are the days when it's safe for them to shinny up ropes or hop through hoops.

It's your responsibility to keep an eye on your older rat and modify her environment to reflect her diminished abilities. Does her balance seem to be off? Then take down the tightrope.

Rats slow down with age.

Is she shaky on her feet? Then steep ladders need to be replaced with gently sloping ramps. You may even need to dismantle a level or two in the cage to keep her safe. Don't expect an elderly rat to do all the tricks she was taught as a youngster—the spirit may be willing but the body's not always able. However, even though your rat may not be up to her old tricks, she still needs quality time and attention. If this means sitting in your lap rather than running the wheel, that's perfectly OK.

Medicine mix

Is your rat sick and needing medication? Is she spitting her daily dose right back at you? Then here's a handy hint. Mix the medication with Nutrical or Ferretvite, and your rat will lap it right up. This tactic works well for most medications. Liquids and small pills can be mixed directly into the good stuff. Large tablets will have to be crushed first. Capsules will have to be opened up and the powdered contents stirred into the Nutrical or Ferretvite.

Housecleaning

Face facts—you can't teach your rats to use a broom and a dustpan. So cage cleaning has to be a training issue for you, not for your rats. By training yourself to clean the cage

A little bit of Nutrical makes the medicine go down.

Rats are prolific poopers—frequent cage cleaning is a must.

regularly, you'll ensure your rats' good health and well-being.

First of all, there's the daily cage maintenance. Thank goodness it's not very time consuming. Take out any table food that might spoil, and wash out water bottles and food dishes. Then, there's scooping the poop. Rats are real little poop machines. If you have several rats in one cage, the poop will pile up in no time. Do you really want your ratties wading through it, eating on it, sleeping in it? Of course not! So do your rats a favor—clean out the droppings daily with an extrasmall cat litter scoop, tweezers, or an old spoon (rat use only, please). This routine takes only a few minutes daily, and you can do it during rat playtime.

Total cage cleaning is a much bigger job. How often should you do it? That depends on the size and type of cage, the number of rats in the cage, and especially the type of bedding used. A good rule of thumb is to clean and disinfect your rats' residence once a week. With some beddings, you'll have to clean more frequently; with others, less frequently. Let your nose be your guide. If you can smell the cage, your rat's probably gagging in it. After all, a rat can out-sniff you any day.

Rub-a-dub-dub

Now that you've done a spit-and-polish job on the cage, how about a little rub-a-dub-dub for the ratties? Rats like to be clean, and they groom themselves frequently throughout the day. However, there's nothing like a good scrub with shampoo to get the fur gleaming. So here are some tub time hints.

Bathing can be done about once a month. Do it more frequently if the bedding you use isn't very efficient at odor control, if you have males with greasy fur, or if your ratties have just had a spaghetti dinner. Put an inch or two of lukewarm water into the tub or the sink. Using a mild baby, kitten, puppy, or ferret shampoo, massage

Rub-a-dub-dub.

Squeaky clean.

each rat gently and rinse well. A brisk rub in a soft, fluffy towel will finish your part of the job. Then watch your rats take over and finish grooming to rat standards.

Finishing off to rat standards.

Between baths, greasy males might need a touch-up. Wring out a washcloth in warm water, add a spot of shampoo, and give their backs a good scrub. Touch-ups won't dry out the skin as much as frequent baths would.

Hygiene hints

Sewer rat, gutter rat, dirty rat—who isn't familiar with these old cliches? But don't worry. You won't catch bubonic plague from your pet. Today's domestic rat is a far cry from the dangerous, disease-carrying pests of the past and from the wild, parasite-infested scavengers of the present. Companion rats, when housed in the home and kept clean, are no more dangerous to your health than a cat or a dog. However, just as with any other pet, when a rat's part of the family, you have to cultivate good hygiene habits.

For example, in the cage, rats walk over their urine and droppings. They also practice coprophagy, which means that they eat some of their feces to obtain certain vitamins. So, to prevent any diseases from being passed to you from your rat, always wash your hands after handling and after playtime.

It's not just your hands that need to be washed after playtime—the play area needs a quick cleanup, too. When the ratties have finished bouncing about the bathroom, wipe the floor with a mild disinfectant. It takes only a minute to ensure good hygiene.

Company's coming

The invitations are out, the company's coming . . . but before you roll out the welcome mat, you need to ask yourself a couple of questions. Will the relatives like the rats? And will the rats like the relatives? If Great Aunt Grace suffers from rattyphobia, it's not a good idea to bring the girls out to say hello. When visitors are afraid of rodents, be considerate and keep your rats right out of sight.

On the other hand, if the nieces and nephews can't wait to get their hands on the rats, be considerate to the rats. Inexperienced rat handlers can cause problems—frightened rats, dropped rats, squeezed rats, stepped-on rats. So either keep the rats out of the limelight, or supervise any rat-handling sessions.

Do your ratties normally roost in the bathroom or the guest room? A few days before the company comes, relocate your pets so that they can adjust to new surroundings. And, if they have to spend extra time in their cage, lavish extra attention on them as often as you can snatch a free moment.

Take these hospitality hints to heart and you, your rats, and your company can all have an enjoyable visit.

Runaways

Even the most careful and conscientious rat owner can make a mistake—a cage door left open, a room door left ajar. Have your ratties flown the coop? Your natural reaction might be to panic. Don't. Swing into action instead.

First, round up any predatory pets in the household, and either put them outside or confine them to their pen or travel cage. Otherwise, your dog, cat, ferret, or parrot might find the ratties before you do. Not good—unless, of course, your dog is buddy-buddy with the rats and can help sniff them out. It's also smart to lock the doors to the outside. You don't want a neighbor walking in and a ratty running out.

Next, call or squeak for the escapees. Start in the room where they vanished, and fan out from there. If you've trained them to answer to their name or to a squeaky toy, they'll probably come running,

Entice a runaway with a food bribe.

especially if they've been on the loose for a while and are getting hungry. However, a recent escapee might be having a whale of a time exploring, and a very frightened rat might be hiding. In either case, you'll have to look in every nook and cranny and listen for any scratching or gnawing. Favorite hiding places are behind the bookcase, beneath the bed, in the closet, under the refrigerator . . . in fact, anywhere you're going to have difficulty getting at them.

When you do locate one of them, how do you convince her to come out? Food bribes are your best bet. Watch out, though, because those little stinkers will often grab the goody right out of your hand and hightail it back to their hiding place. Runaway rats are like greased lightening!

If squeaking and outright bribery don't work, try sitting quietly near their hideout and see if the fugitives come to you. Or try positioning their cage nearby. When they're hungry or thirsty, they might make for familiar ground. Should you have a rat in hand, even better. Use her as a decoy. Put her into the cage, and give her crunchy treats to munch. At the sound of the chomping, the other runaways will very likely come to claim their share.

When the adventure has lost it's novelty, most well-trained rats will be happy to come to you. But if all else fails, you can move the furniture (a pain at 3:00 A.M.) or invest in a live small-animal trap.

Chapter Fifteen
Lifetime Learning

The well-schooled rat

Congratulations! You've made the grade! Or, rather, with your help, those rambunctious ratties have made the grade. Of course, training has taken time, patience, and effort . . . but hasn't it been time well spent?

Now, instead of being skittish or standoffish, your pets are easygoing and all-over-you friendly. Now, instead of giving you blank looks when you call their names, they give you instant attention when you squeeze that old squeaky toy. And, instead of sleeping their days away, your rats are keeping body and brain on the ball by cavorting in a custom-fitted cage or exercising in a rat-proofed room.

Keep it up!

It's tempting to pat yourself on the back and rest on your laurels. But don't. After all, do you want those well-schooled rats forgetting what they've learned? Training is an ongoing job. You have to keep up the practice and rewards if you expect the rats to keep up the learned behaviors. You also have to introduce new challenges if you expect the rats to stay on their toes.

For happy, healthy rats, training is the way to go. It's the way to guarantee that your rats have the best possible quality of life. And isn't that something every ratty deserves?

The well-schooled rat, alert and ready for action.

Useful Literature and Addresses

Rat organizations

American Fancy Rat and Mouse
  Association (AFRMA)
P.O. Box 2589
Winnetka, CA 91396-2589
Web site: www.afrma.org

National Fancy Rat Society (NFRS)
P.O. Box 24207
London SE9 5ZS England
Web site: www.cableol.co.uk/nfrs

Northamerican Rat & Mouse Club
  International
219 Oakwood Avenue
Glassboro, NJ 08028
Web site:
  www.angelfire.com/nj2/nrmci

Rat and Mouse Club of America
  (RMCA)
13075 Springdale Street #302
Westminster, CA 92683
Web site: www.rmca.org

Rat Fan Club
Debbie "The Rat Lady" Ducommun
P.O. Box 6794
Chico, CA 92927-6794
e-mail: Debbietheratlady@juno.com
Web site: www.ratfanclub.org

Books

*Fancy Rats–A Complete Pet
  Owner's Manual*
Gisela Bulla
Barron's Educational Series, Inc.,
  1999
250 Wireless Boulevard
Hauppauge, NY 11788

Guide to Owning a Rat
Susan Fox
TFH Publications, Inc., 1996
1 TFH Plaza
Neptune, NJ 07753

Rats! A Fun and Care Book
Debbie Ducommun
Bowtie Press, 1998
3 Burroughs
Irvine, CA 92618

*Rats–A Complete Pet Owner's
  Manual*
Carol A. Himsel, D.V.M.
Barron's Educational Series, Inc.,
  1991
250 Wireless Boulevard
Hauppauge, NY 11788

The Rat—An Owner's Guide to a
    Happy, Healthy Pet
Howell Book House, 1997
Simon & Schuster/MacMillan
    Publishing
1633 Broadway
New York, NY 10019

Periodicals

The Rat and Mouse Gazette
Published by the Rat and Mouse
    Club of America
13075 Springdale Street
Suite 302
Westminster, CA 92683

Rat and Mouse Tales
Published by the American Fancy
    Rat and Mouse Association
P.O. Box 2589
Winnetka, CA 91396-2589

Pro-Rat-A
Published by the National
    Fancy Rat Society
P.O. Box 24207
London SE9 5ZS England

The Rat Report
Published by the Rat Fan Club
P.O. Box 6794
Chico, CA 92927-6794

Critters USA
Published by Fancy Publications
P.O. Box 6050
Mission Viejo, CA 92690

Index